H. Norman Wright

Starting
Out
Together

A Devotional for Dating
or Engaged Couples

H. NORMAN WRIGHT

Starting Out Together

A DEVOTIONAL FOR DATING OR ENGAGED COUPLES

BETHANYHOUSE
a division of Baker Publishing Group
Minneapolis, Minnesota

© 1996 by H. Norman Wright

Published by Bethany House Publishers
11400 Hampshire Avenue South
Bloomington, Minnesota 55438
www.bethanyhouse.com

Bethany House Publishers is a division of
Baker Publishing Group, Grand Rapids, Michigan

Bethany House edition published 2014
ISBN 978-0-7642-1656-5

Previously published by Regal Books

Printed in the United States of America

The Library of Congress has cataloged the original edition as follows:
Wright, H. Norman
        Starting out together : dating or engaged couples devotional /
H. Norman Wright.
        p. cm.
        Includes bibliographical references.
        ISBN 0-8307-1901-6 (trade paper)
BV4596.M3W47 1996
248.8'44—dc20   96-26299

Contents

Introduction

Marriage—the wonder of it all. You are probably, and hopefully, pretty excited right now. You are about to embark on one of the greatest and longest journeys of your life. I am sure you have dreams for your marriage relationship. Every couple does. Some will be realized and some will not. That is part of the journey.

During the past 35 years of working with couples, many have asked: "What one suggestion would you give us to help us have the marriage we want?" My answer is simple— build your marriage upon Jesus Christ and develop a depth of spiritual intimacy in your relationship.

Spiritual boundary. Spiritual intimacy. Spiritual closeness. This is the foundation for your life together. How close are you spiritually right at this moment? Have you learned to pray together? Have you discussed in depth your beliefs yet? Have you learned to share and apply God's Word to your relationship?

It is possible for you to grow spiritually together even before you are married. That is what this book is all about. Take a few minutes each day to read a selection aloud to one another. Think about what you have read and then discuss it together. You may be amazed at the results.

You will probably complete this book before you marry; and that is all right. It will be the beginning of your spiritual journey together. Let me encourage you to continue this practice after you marry. Two other resources are available for you to use during the next few years: *Quiet Times for Couples* and then later *Quiet Times for Parents* (both by Harvest House).

May God guide you and bless you as you seek to grow together in Him.

H. Norman Wright

The Commitments of Marriage

COMMIT YOUR WAY TO THE LORD, TRUST ALSO IN HIM.

Psalm 37:5 (NASB)

Your marriage—a lifetime of memories.

As you approach your marriage, you are beginning the entry to a lifetime of memories. Years from now you will be amazed at the memories you have accumulated. Not only the quantity of memories is important, but also the quality. What will make the difference in the quality of the memories you gather? One simple word—commitment.

"Commitment" is just one simple 10-letter word; but it's a costly word. It can bring peace, maturity and stability, but at the same time it can also bring tension, and sometimes questions as well.

During the 1800s in Hawaii, the government developed a policy to take care of those who were afflicted with leprosy. They were sent to the island of Molokai to live their remaining days in isolation. The policy was: out of sight, out of mind. The afflicted were allowed, however, to be accompanied by a *Kokua*—a person who chose to go with them and be with them for the rest of their lives until the leprous person died. If the Kokua had not contracted the disease, he or she was then allowed to return home. If leprosy had been contracted, however, the Kokua remained in Molokai until death.

In James Michener's book *Hawaii*, the story is told of a man who noticed a numbness setting into his toes and fingers. In time, he knew what it was. One evening after dinner he told his wife and children he had leprosy. His wife looked at him and said, "I will be your Kokua." This is the substance of marital commitment.

What are the commitments you need to make in your marriage?

As you walk through life, which brings rapid, unexpected changes, unfairness, tragedy and unanswered questions, commitment to living by faith will guide you through the journey.

Commit your life to the person of Jesus Christ, who is the Son of God. Make this a daily decision together.

Commit your life to the Word of God, which brings stability and peace. Read the Word daily together.

Commit yourself to seeing your partner as having worth, value, and dignity because God sent His Son to die for him or her. Remind yourself of this daily.

Commit yourselves as a couple to prayer. No greater intimacy can occur than when you open your hearts to God together. This will enhance your completeness and oneness as well as help put your differences and adjustments into a better perspective. When the lines are open to God, they are invariably open to one another. You cannot be genuinely open to God and closed to your partner.

Commit your life to giving your marriage top priority in terms of time, energy, thought and planning for growth.

Commit yourself to a life of fidelity and faithfulness, regardless of your feelings or the lure of life around you.

Commit and open yourself to the working of the Holy Spirit in your life.

"When the Holy Spirit controls our lives he will produce this kind of fruit in us: love, joy, peace, patience, kindness, goodness, faithfulness, gentleness and self-control" (Gal. 5:22,23, *TLB*).

Faith, hope and love will grow out of your commitment to one another and to God and His Word.

Follow this advice and you will gather memories.[1]

Note
1. H. Norman Wright, *Quiet Times for Parents* (Eugene, Oreg.: Harvest House Publishers, 1995), September 2, adapted.

Vulnerability in Marriage

NOW THE LORD GOD SAID, IT IS NOT GOOD (SUFFI-
CIENT, SATISFACTORY) THAT THE MAN SHOULD BE
ALONE; I WILL MAKE HIM A HELPER MEET (SUITABLE,
ADAPTED, COMPLEMENTARY) FOR HIM.

Genesis 2:18 (Amp.)

The very first thing God declared "not good" was being alone. We were not created to live in isolation, for the pain of it is insufferable. Loneliness carries with it one of the greatest sources of pain in life. The choice to be married is a decision not to live in isolation and loneliness. Some who are married, however, eventually do live in loneliness. This loneliness is overwhelming. Be sure you are able to connect, relate and be vulnerable. Accept the fact that being open carries with it a risk—of being hurt.

There is the risk of being misunderstood—but if so, it can be resolved. There is the risk of not being accepted—perhaps, but perhaps not. There is the risk of being laughed at—true, but the other person usually laughs with you. There is the risk of having to face who you really are—that's good, but it is better for you to confront it before marriage than to surprise your partner with your insecurities after marriage.

When you open the door of your heart and mind to reveal to your partner who you really are, and perhaps what you have never revealed before, you have taken a step to forbid loneliness to seep into your relationship. When each of you shares this openly with one another, treat what you have received as special and fragile.

If you don't risk, the alternative is to live your life in fear and hiding. We weren't called to have that kind of lifestyle, especially in marriage. Remember Adam? He tried to hide from God. It didn't work. It won't work in marriage either.

Being vulnerable and open with your partner holds the potential for much joy, many hopes, much satisfaction and happiness, much laughter, much comfort, support and a fulfilling life. Why would anyone want to avoid it?

Being vulnerable and open is like transversing a path through a dimly lit narrow cave, and then discovering a brilliantly illuminated cavern containing an open treasure chest sitting in the middle of the floor. As you remove each item, you discover something new. The chest is never emptied.

That's the way your marriage is to become. A stream of constant discoveries that enhances you, your partner and your relationship—and it begins with you. Never hold back—reveal. After all, isn't that what God did as He sought you?

Elements That Will Make Your Marriage Work

HE WHO HEEDS INSTRUCTION AND CORRECTION IS
[NOT ONLY HIMSELF] IN THE WAY OF LIFE [BUT ALSO]
IS A WAY OF LIFE FOR OTHERS.

Proverbs 10:17 (Amp.)

THE BEGINNING OF WISDOM IS: GET WISDOM.

Proverbs 4:7 (Amp.)

The following are random thoughts gathered from more than 35 years of marriage and from 30 years of counseling couples. I hope learning these principles now, rather than painfully discovering them through unwanted experiences, will make your marital journey easier and more fulfilling.

When you marry, each of you will be assuming two different roles. At times you will become a teacher to your partner, instructing information and experience the person is lacking. Remember that a wise teacher doesn't force or always tell, but leads a student to discover things personally, which enhances the desire to learn. At times you will assume the role of a student and your life will be enhanced by what you learn from your partner. Remember that a real learner is one who is open to consider different views, is not resistant and admits a need to learn. When both of you can do this, watch your relationship grow!

We live in a competitive society. Sometimes competing is necessary, but never compete with one another. There is no place for competition in marriage. You will at times disagree. That's normal and healthy, but behaving disagreeably isn't necessary. When differences appear in your relationship, your goal is reconciliation, not blame. Learn from each disagreement so it is resolved rather than repeated.

Your partner will say or do some things that will bother you. Be sure to tell your partner what you would like him or her to do, rather than to concentrate on what you don't like. This will likely cause your partner to respond as you desire the next time.

Remember how you fell in love? You talked, you listened and you did loving acts. You will stay in love by not only continuing to do those very things, but also by doing them with a higher level of frequency and intensity than you did before. Don't let these acts diminish or be extinguished.

Always be supportive and loyal to one another. Put into practice 1 Corinthians 13:7: "If you love someone you will be loyal to him no matter what the cost. You will always believe in him, always expect the best of him, and always stand your ground in defending him" *(TLB)*. Give one another the benefit of the doubt.

When conflicts arise, don't avoid them. If you do, you will just bury the problem and you'll have buried it alive. Eventually it will rise from its grave and confront you. If you want to get rid of your conflicts, look them squarely in the face, talk about them and discover creative ways to resolve them. Learn from them. Use them as growth experiences.

A gentle hug or holding one another in silence is an act of love that conveys the message, *You're special. I love you. I understand.* It's a daily act. It's like God's message to us of His love; it's continuous.[1]

Note
1. H. Norman Wright, *Quiet Times for Parents* (Eugene, Oreg.: Harvest House Publishers, 1995), November 2, adapted.

Friendship Love

HIS MOUTH IS SWEETNESS ITSELF; HE IS ALTOGETHER
LOVELY. THIS IS MY LOVER, THIS MY FRIEND,
O DAUGHTERS OF JERUSALEM.

Song of Songs 5:16

Marriage includes many dimensions of love. One of the most important is friendship. What does friendship love entail? It is an unselfish dedication to your partner's happiness. It is when fulfilling your partner's needs becomes one of your needs. It is learning to enjoy what your partner enjoys, not just to convince him or her that you are the right person, but to *develop the enjoyment yourself as you share the enjoyment together.*

Your friendship will mean you can enjoy some aspects of life together, but you are also comfortable having your own individual interests. You don't resent your partner's enjoyment, although it is the last thing you would ever want to do! Be sure you encourage each other in separate endeavors. It is important to maintain a balance between togetherness and separateness.

Be willing to try the activities your partner enjoys, but understanding that you have the freedom to enjoy them or not to enjoy them, to continue or to discontinue them.

If you want the other person to learn your own enjoyable activity, it may help to cut back the time and intensity of your involvement in it when introducing it. This helps to make it more comfortable for the other person to experience it. After all, it is difficult for an amateur to keep up with a pro!

Friendship love also involves a certain level of intimacy in which there is openness, vulnerability and emotional connection. Be sure to share your goals, plans and dreams, and work together on them. Never become a stranger to your partner in any area of life.

Remember, marriages that last are marriages in which a husband and wife are friends. As your friendship develops through the years, you will discover that you chose each other for just the joy of the other person's company. You just like being together.

Be sure to practice your friendship. Friendship is part of God's intention for marriage and should include a vow of trust. Don't become selfishly competitive, but wish your partner the best. You should share each other's happiness and rejoice in it almost as much as the other person does.

A friend does not automatically approve of everything we do or say, and that's all right. True friends don't attempt to control each other because they respect each other too much. Friends try to understand the other person's preferences. They learn to say, "What do you think?" and, "What do you want to do?" Becoming a friend necessitates changing old habits and beliefs; and that too is all right. Friendship causes you to become a more balanced and mature person. God will use your partner to reshape you. Learn to enjoy the improvements; they will benefit both of you.[1]

Note
1. H. Norman Wright, *Quiet Times for Parents* (Eugene, Oreg.: Harvest House Publishers, 1995), October 22, adapted.

Servanthood in Marriage

SUBMIT TO ONE ANOTHER OUT OF
REVERENCE FOR CHRIST.

Ephesians 5:21

Marriage involves an act of abandonment. In its simplest form, it means you cannot take your single lifestyle into your marriage. You can no longer think as a single person. The word "we" replaces "I." You can no longer respond, plan, play or have the involvements of a single person. Every aspect of your life will be shared, from the dresser drawers, closet and bathroom to the way you spend your money and plan for the yearly vacation. Your calling now is together-ness, and that involves making life easier for your partner rather than creating more work. You are now adopting the role of a servant. Christ calls you to serve Him and one another.

In a marriage relationship, being a servant is an act of love, a gift to your partner to make his or her life fuller. It is an act of strength and not of weakness. It is a positive action that has been chosen to show your love to each other. The apostle Paul said, "Submit to one another" (Eph. 5:21)—don't limit the role of servanthood to a wife. It is meant for both of you.

A servant may also be called an "enabler," in the good sense of the word, which means "to make better." As an enabler you are to make life easier for your partner instead of placing restrictive demands upon him or her.

A servant is also someone who edifies another person.

In the New Testament, to edify someone often refers to building up another person. Do you know how you will do this throughout the years of your marriage? Take the following verses into your heart and practice them each day:

> Let us then definitely aim for and eagerly pursue
> what makes for harmony and for mutual upbuild-

ing (edification and development) of one another
(Rom. 14:19, *Amp.*).

Let each one of us make it a practice to please
(make happy) his neighbor for his good and for his
true welfare, to edify him [to strengthen him and
build him up spiritually] (Rom. 15:2, *Amp.*).

Encourage one another and build each other up
(1 Thess. 5:11).

First Corinthians 8:1 sums up the matter of edifying:
"Love builds up."

That is your calling—never tear down, don't just maintain, but always build up.

When you follow this advice, it won't matter at all that
you gave up your single life. Look at what you gained. It can
be far more than you ever imagined!

Some Wisdom About Marriage

DEATH AND LIFE ARE IN THE POWER OF THE TONGUE,
AND THEY WHO INDULGE IN IT SHALL EAT THE FRUIT
OF IT [FOR DEATH OR LIFE].

Proverbs 18:21 (Amp.)

A WORD FITLY SPOKEN AND IN DUE SEASON IS LIKE
APPLES OF GOLD IN A SETTING OF SILVER.

Proverbs 25:11 (Amp.)

As you are about to embark upon your marriage, consider the following thoughts about this journey from the pen of Richard Exley and his wisdom.

Getting married is wonderful and also scary. A marriage may be made in heaven, but the maintenance must be done on earth. May you always consider each other first, before others.

Don't destroy each other with words, especially in public. Words are very powerful, they can kill love faster than roses can mend it. Always work toward the best for each other. Never leave each other without a kiss or an "I love you." Three little words, but they mean so much. Respect each other or the stars won't come out at night. Even in a crowd always let each other know you are aware of them.

Romance is a fragile flower, and it cannot long survive where it is ignored or taken for granted. Without commitment and imagination, it will slowly wither and die. But for those who are committed to keeping romance in their marriage, the best is yet to come.

Marriage is what you make it. Under God, it must be the most important relationship in all your life. If your marriage is good, you can overcome any-thing—financial adversity, illness, rejection, anything. If it is not good, there is not enough success in the world to fill the awful void. Remember, nothing, absolutely nothing, is more important than your marriage, so work at it with love and thoughtfulness all the days of your life.

Guard it against all intruders. Remember your vows. You have promised, before God and your families, to forsake all others and cleave only to each other. Never allow friends, or family, or work or anything else to come between you and your beloved.

Marriage is made of time, so schedule time together. Spend it wisely in deep sharing. Listen carefully and with understanding when he in turn shares his heart with you. Spend it wisely in fun—laugh and play together. Go places and do things together. Spend it wisely in worship—pray together. Spend it wisely in touching—hold each other—be affectionate.[1]

How will you remember to follow these words in your marriage? It is something to think about.

Note
1. Richard Exley, *Straight from the Heart for Couples* (Tulsa, Okla.: Honor Books, 1993), pp. 21, 22, 57, 69, 72.

£isten to One Another

HE WHO GIVES AN ANSWER BEFORE HE HEARS,

IT IS FOLLY AND SHAME TO HIM.

Proverbs 18:13 (NASB)

As you look toward your wedding day and a lifetime of marriage, one ingredient will need constant attention for your relationship to flourish. I think you already know what it is—communication. You may think you are communicating now. To a certain degree you are communicating; but the two of you haven't yet learned to really speak one another's language. In some ways, each of you is still somewhat of a foreigner to each other. Learn to use your partner's style of thinking and speaking when the two of you interact together. This will help you to understand and to draw closer to each other.

Remember that communication is not only talking, but also silence, a quiet look, a gentle touch.

Discover the best time of the day for each of you to communicate and give each other the gift of your individual attention. Set aside a bit of time each day to sit together, hold hands and share your hearts and your deepest feelings. Make the first four minutes you see one another at the end of the day's work a time of positive interaction through touch and talking.

Do more than talk; listen as well. Listen with your mind, heart, ears and eyes. Remember that nonverbal language can say more than words can. Listening styles also differ, especially between men and women. Practice the principles of God's Word in your listening. "I love the Lord, because He hears my voice and my supplications. Because He has inclined His ear to me, therefore I shall call upon Him as long as I live" (Ps. 116:1,2, *NASB*).

True listening requires total attention, no distractions, and not letting your mind formulate what you will say as soon as your partner stops talking. One of the greatest gifts you can give is to listen. Too many discussions become dialogues of the deaf. "Let every man be quick to hear [a ready listener]" (Jas. 1:19, *Amp.*). Ask your partner when is the best time of the day to talk to each other.

Consider the following words someone penned years ago (source unknown):

"When I ask you to listen to me and you start giving advice, you have not done what I asked.

"When I ask you to listen to me and you begin to tell me why I shouldn't feel that way, you are trampling on my feelings. When I ask you to listen to me and you feel you have to do something to solve my problems, you have failed me, strange as that may seem.

"So please, just listen a few minutes for your turn and I promise I'll listen to you."

Above all, remember who it is who never tires of listening to you.

A Prayer for Your Marriage

IF I GIVE ALL I POSSESS TO THE POOR AND
SURRENDER MY BODY TO THE FLAMES,
BUT HAVE NOT LOVE, I GAIN NOTHING.

1 Corinthians 13:3

When you marry, you will need to take along some
resources that will enable you to complete the journey.
They need to be resources that will endure as well as provide you with ongoing strength. The following passage
and prayer will be a helpful resource. After you have read
the passage, refer to each section and talk about what each
phrase means to you and how you will practice it in your
relationship.

Lord, we believe that You ordained marriage and
that You also sustain it.

Help us to exercise faith.
Faith that You answer prayer
    and heal wounded hearts.
Faith that You forgive and restore.
Faith that Your hand of love
    will clasp our hands together.
Faith that You build bridges of reconciliation.
Faith that all things will work for good
    to those who love You.

Help us to hold on to hope.
Hope that enables us to endure
    times of trial and testing.
Hope that fixes our gaze on possibilities
    rather than problems.
Hope that focuses on the road ahead
    instead of detours already passed.

Hope that instills trust, even in the midst
   of failure.
Hope that harbors happiness.

Help us to lift up love.
Love that doesn't falter or faint
   in the winds of adversity.
Love that is determined to grow and bear fruit.
Love that is slow to anger and quick to praise.
Love that looks for ways of saying,
   "I care for you."
Love that remains steady during shaky days.

Lord, may Your gifts of faith, hope and love find plenty of living room in our hearts. Thank You that these three abide—and the greatest is love. Make our home an outpost for Your kingdom and an oasis for wandering pilgrims. In the name of Jesus who blessed the marriage at Cana with a miracle. Amen.[1]

Note
1. Reprinted from "Forty Ways to Say I Love You" by James R. Bjorge (Minneapolis, Minn.: Augsburg Publishing House, 1978), pp. 91-92. Used by permission of Augsburg Press.

It Takes Character

AND ENDURANCE (FORTITUDE) DEVELOPS MATURITY
OF CHARACTER (APPROVED FAITH AND TRIED
INTEGRITY). AND CHARACTER [OF THIS SORT]
PRODUCES [THE HABIT OF] JOYFUL AND
CONFIDENT HOPE OF ETERNAL SALVATION.

Romans 5:4 (Amp.)

You need to bring many qualities to your marriage for it to work. One of these qualities is character. Some people *are* "characters" and others *have* character. The latter is the needed quality. It may not sound all that romantic or as much fun as some other qualities, but its staying power will hold the structure of your marriage together. Do you know what the dictionary says about character? It describes it as a distinctive trait, quality or attribute, moral strength, self-discipline, fortitude.[1]

Good character isn't fickle. A person can be counted on to persevere during the hard times, and be consistently dependable, not flaky. The person is not as James describes, "being a double-minded man, unstable in all his ways" (1:8, *NASB*).

When the relationship experiences hard times and is shaken, a man or woman of character stays. The person doesn't think of the possibility of escaping. Those who have character will take their vows very seriously on the wedding day. Character believes every word of the vows with the whole heart and being. Character means never saying: "I didn't know what I was doing" or "I didn't mean them" or "I changed my mind." Character believes a promise is a promise, and a commitment is just that. Psalm 15 talks about the qualities of a godly man, and one of them is: "keeps a promise even if it ruins him" (v. 4, *TLB*).

You probably have no concept of what it really means when you repeat those vows: "In sickness and in health, for richer and for poorer." You will, though. At some point in your marriage, you will. The depth of your character will keep you going. Marriage is not something you try just to see if you like it or not. Marriage has no revolving door, no return policy and no escape clause *when* you find the defects in your partner. It should not be treated as a "starter marriage," as though purchasing a "starter house" and then selling it to move on to a new model. In marriage, you just keep adding on and making home improvements.

Marriage is not for the overly independent, or for the isolate, the controller, the irresponsible or the immature. That's strong language, isn't it? It was meant to be. Marriage is too serious, too sacred, to be taken lightly. God did not create the marriage relationship for those who can't keep track of time, can't be home when promised, don't inform a partner when expecting to be late, forget important dates such as anniversaries and birthdays, or don't let a partner know about thoughts or plans. God created marriage for those who possess character. And that's you—isn't it?

Note
1. *Webster's New World Dictionary,* Third Edition (New York: Prentice Hall, 1995), p. 235.

Handling Frustration in Marriage

A PATIENT MAN HAS GREAT UNDERSTANDING, BUT
A QUICK-TEMPERED MAN DISPLAYS FOLLY.

Proverbs 14:29

Welcome to the world of frustration—marriage. You have probably experienced some frustration already; but just wait until you start planning the details of the wedding. Then you can relax—or can you? Frustrations will occur more than you realize once you are married; and some of them will flare into anger.

What culprits create frustration? One will be your expectations. We all have expectations, but some have more than others have. You have expectations for yourself, your friends, your soon-to-be partner and now for your marriage relationship. One problem: Too many expectations remain unspoken. When this happens, expectations may turn into demands.

You cannot expect your partner to read your mind and just "know" what you expect. You cannot expect your partner to be exactly like an idolized parent, or totally unlike the parent. You may expect your partner to supply all you missed as a child. This puts pressure on your partner and will only result in one thing—frustration.

Another cause for frustration is a belief or value from the baby boomer generation—it is called "entitlement." This belief says if you want something, the other person has no right to say no. It confuses desire with obligation. Unfortunately, this mind-set says your partner must give up his or her boundaries for you. It is another form of demanding. This attitude shows little care or concern for a partner. What happens when your partner brings the same attitude into the marriage? The result may be a standoff, a clash, a power struggle and frustration. An attitude of entitlement is doomed to failure; not only won't it work, but it is also contrary to the teaching of Scripture.

Another reason for frustration developing in marriage is the belief that life must be fair. Relationships must be fair and my partner must be fair according to my standard of fairness.

Who determines what is fair? Who said life is fair? If you want to be frustrated, hold on to this belief. It will get you there fast! Keep in mind that frustration doesn't remain frustration; it evolves into anger. Sometimes your anger emerges because you want a better, closer, more intimate relationship with your partner. That's okay, but remember—responding in frustration and anger won't draw you closer, but will create a greater distance between you. After all, who wants to come close to a frustrated angry partner?

What can you do to keep the frustration out of your marriage? Identify your expectations, evaluate them and discuss them. Evict the feelings of entitlement in your life. Who wants to keep a belief that is doomed to failure? Do the same with the belief that life must be fair.

Then, internalize the guidelines from God's Word. God has preserved those Scriptures through the centuries for a major reason: His guidelines for life are the best because they work.

Read the following two fundamental truths from Proverbs. Memorize them, practice them and watch your frustration shrink:

A wise man controls his temper. He knows that anger causes mistakes (14:29, *TLB*).

It is better to be slow-tempered than famous; it is better to have self-control than to control an army (16:32, *TLB*).

Forgiveness in Marriage

HE WHO COVERS AND FORGIVES AN OFFENSE SEEKS
LOVE, BUT HE WHO REPEATS OR HARPS ON A MATTER
SEPARATES EVEN CLOSE FRIENDS.

Proverbs 17:9 (Amp.)

After you are married, a day will come when you will need to practice one of the elements of God's grace to all of us— forgiveness. I would like to be honest with you: Some days you won't think your partner deserves your forgiveness. That is all right; it is nothing new. None of us deserve the forgiveness we receive.

Sometimes you may find it hard to forgive the one you are about to marry. You may be concerned that by forgiving your partner you are letting him or her off the hook and that what happened may reoccur. That is a risk you have to take. After all, the only other option is resentment and revenge.

Do you know about resentment and revenge? The resentful heart operates like a bill-collection agency, making the person pay again and again for what we believe he or she has done. We often charge so much interest, however, that no matter how earnestly the other person tries to pay the debt, a balance always seems to be held against the person. Resentment costs both parties; it hurts the offender and the offendee. The greatest damage, however, is done to the relationship.

In marriage, there will always be disappointments, hurts and unmet needs and expectations. After all, you will marry an imperfect person—and, incidentally, so will your partner! Instead of forgiving a spouse's failures, the resenting spouse says, "You hurt me! You owe me! You must pay! I will get even with you!" But you can never get even.[1]

Forgiveness hurts. It is rare because it is hard. It will cost you love and pride. Pain is involved. But eventually it will diminish. Forgiveness is also costly because when you forgive, you are saying to your partner, "You don't have to make up to me for what you did." You are actually releasing your partner and reaching out in love instead of relishing resentments. It means not allowing the other person to pay.

When you have truly forgiven your partner, you never have a need to discuss the problem, believe it is going to happen again or dwell on it again!

A mature marriage is a forgiving marriage. Be sure to verbalize the phrases, "Will you forgive me?" as well as, "I forgive you." You know you have what it takes to forgive one another—anyone who knows Jesus as Savior has been given that power. You have been loved, accepted and forgiven by God. So the gift given to you is yours to use with other people.

If you wonder whether you have truly forgiven your spouse, just keep this in mind: You have forgiven your partner when in your heart you wish him or her well and are able to ask God's blessing upon his or her life.

Our greatest example of forgiveness is the cross of Jesus Christ. God chose the Cross as the way of reconciliation.

> For you have been called for this purpose, since Christ also suffered for you, leaving you an example for you to follow in His steps (1 Pet. 2:21, *NASB*).
>
> He himself bore our sins...on the tree (1 Pet. 2:24, *RSV*).

We are called to forgive as God has forgiven us.

> Be as ready to forgive others as God for Christ's sake has forgiven you (Eph. 4:32, *Phillips*).

Note
1. H. Norman Wright, *Quiet Times for Parents* (Eugene, Oreg.: Harvest House Publishers, 1995), p. 104, adapted.

How to Pray in Marriage

IN THE SAME WAY, THE SPIRIT HELPS US IN OUR
WEAKNESS. WE DO NOT KNOW WHAT WE OUGHT TO
PRAY FOR, BUT THE SPIRIT HIMSELF INTERCEDES FOR
US WITH GROANS THAT WORDS CANNOT EXPRESS.

Romans 8:26

Have you ever felt like this when it comes to prayer?—"I just don't know what to say when I pray. Sometimes I'm at a loss for words."

If you've ever felt this way, you're not alone. We've all felt like this at some point.

> The Spirit of God...helps us in our present limita-
> tions. For example, we *do not* know how to pray
> worthily as sons of God, but his Spirit within us is
> actually praying for us in those agonizing long-
> ings which never find words. And God who
> knows the heart's secrets understands, of course,
> the Spirit's intention as he prays for those who
> love God (Rom. 8:26,27, *Phillips*, emphasis mine).

The Holy Spirit is God's answer when we don't know how to pray. You and I cannot pray as we ought to pray. We are often crippled in our prayer lives. That's where the work of the Holy Spirit really comes into play. He helps us in our prayer lives by showing us what we should pray for and how we ought to pray. That's quite a promise.

One of your callings in marriage is to assist your partner when he or she needs help. You are always to be listening for a call for assistance. Similarly, there is someone looking out for us when we need help in our prayer lives: the Holy Spirit. There are several specific ways that He helps us.

First, *the Spirit intercedes for you* when you are oppressed by problems in life or when you feel down on yourself. He brings you to the place where you can pray. Your ability to begin praying is prompted and produced by the working of the Holy Spirit within you.

Second, *the Spirit reveals to your mind what you should pray for.* He makes you conscious of such things as your needs, your lack of faith, your fears, your need to be obedient, etc. He helps you identify your spiritual needs and bring them into the presence of God. He helps you by diminishing your fears, increasing your faith, and strengthening your hope. If you're at a loss to know what you need to pray for about your partner or even what to pray for together, ask the Holy Spirit to intercede for you.

Third, *the Spirit guides you by directing your thoughts* to the promises of God's Word that are best suited to your needs. He helps you realize the truth of God's promises. The discernment that you lack on your own is supplied to you by the Spirit. Perhaps you're looking for a verse to apply to your marriage. Again, help is available through the Spirit.

Finally, *the Spirit helps you pray in the right way.* He helps you sift through your prayers and bring them into conformity with the purpose of prayer.

When you experience a crisis, it may be difficult for you to talk. But you and your spouse can hold each other in your arms and quietly allow the Holy Spirit to pray for you. This is called the silent prayer of the heart.

When you are having difficulty praying, remember that you have someone to draw on for strength in developing your prayer life.[1]

Note
1. H. Norman Wright, *The Secrets of a Lasting Marriage* (Ventura, Calif.: Regal Books, 1995), pp. 162-163.

Do You Want an Intimate Marriage?

THE LORD GOD SAID, "IT IS NOT GOOD FOR
THE MAN TO BE ALONE. I WILL MAKE A HELPER
SUITABLE FOR HIM."

Genesis 2:18

Intimacy is the glue that will hold your marriage together. But do you know what it is? It's not just sex—that's just one expression of it. And you can have sex without intimacy. The dictionary conveys the ideas that follow.

> Intimacy suggests a very strong personal relationship, a special emotional closeness that includes understanding and being understood by someone who is very special. Intimacy has also been defined as an affectionate bond, the strands of which are composed of mutual caring, responsibility, trust, open communication of feelings and sensations, and the nondefended interchange of information about significant emotional events. Intimacy means taking the risk to be close to someone and allowing that someone to step inside your personal boundaries.
>
> Sometimes intimacy can hurt. As you lower your defenses to let each other close, you reveal the real, intimate, secret *you* to each other, including your weaknesses and faults. With the real you exposed, you become vulnerable to possible ridicule from your partner. The risk of pain is there, but the rewards of intimacy greatly overshadow the risk.
>
> Although intimacy means vulnerability, it also means security. The openness can be scary, but the acceptance each partner offers in the midst of vulnerability provides a wonderful sense of security.

Intimate couples can feel safe and accepted—fully exposed perhaps, yet fully accepted.

Intimacy can occur outside of marriage commitment and without the element of physical love. Women can be intimate with women and men with men. The closeness of intimacy involves private and personal interaction, commitment, and caring. We can speak of intimacy between friends as well as intimacy between spouses.

Intimacy can exist without marriage, but it is impossible for a meaningful marriage to exist without intimacy. For two hearts to touch each other, intimacy is a must. If you don't know how your partner thinks and feels about various issues or concerns, he or she is somewhat of a stranger to you. And for two hearts to be bonded together, they cannot be strangers.

It is often assumed that intimacy automatically occurs between married partners. But I've seen far too many "married strangers." I've talked to too many husbands and wives who feel isolated from their spouses and lonely even after many years of marriage. I've heard statements like:

"We share the same house, the same table, and the same bed, but we might as well be strangers."

"We've lived together for twenty-three years, and yet I don't know my spouse any better now than when we married."

"What really hurts is that we can spend a weekend together and I still feel lonely. I think I married someone who would have preferred being a hermit in some ways."

No, intimacy is not automatic.[1]

Note
1. H. Norman Wright, *The Secrets of a Lasting Marriage* (Ventura, Calif.: Regal Books, 1995), p. 152.

The Dimensions of Intimacy

HIS VOICE AND SPEECH ARE EXCEEDINGLY
SWEET; YES, HE IS ALTOGETHER LOVELY
[THE WHOLE OF HIM DELIGHTS AND IS PRECIOUS].
THIS IS MY BELOVED, AND THIS IS MY FRIEND,
O DAUGHTERS OF JERUSALEM!

Song of Solomon 5:16 (Amp.)

What comes to mind when the word "intimacy" is mentioned? Sex? That is okay. Many think of it that way. But there is more than one definition of intimacy.

Several elements are involved in creating an intimate relationship. Many relationships have gaps in them for one reason or another. You may be close in two or three areas but distant in others. If you feel you have a close, intimate relationship, but you're distant in a couple of them or even one, there is work to be done. Let's consider the various dimensions...because they all relate.

Emotional intimacy is the foundation for relating in a couple's relationship. There is a "feeling" of closeness when this exists, a mutual feeling of care and support coming from each person. You share everything in the emotional arena, including your hurts and your joys. You understand each other, and you're attentive to your partner's feelings.

Social intimacy involves having friends in common rather than always socializing separately. Having mutual friends to play with, talk with, pray with and give reciprocal support to is reflective of this important dimension.

Sexual intimacy is taken for granted in marriage. Many couples have sex but no sexual intimacy. Performing a physical act is one thing, but communicating about it is another. Sexual intimacy involves satisfaction with what occurs. But it also means you talk about it, endeavor to meet your partner's needs, and keep it from being routine. There is an understanding of each other's unique gender needs, and flexibility in meeting them.

There is even the dimension of *intellectual* intimacy—the sharing of ideas and the stimulation of each other's level of knowledge and understanding. You are each different, and you have grown because of what your partner has shared with you.

Recreational intimacy means you share and enjoy the same interests and activities. You just like to play together, and it doesn't have to be competitive. You have fun together, and it draws you closer together.

For a couple to have spiritual intimacy they need shared beliefs as to who Jesus is and the basic tenets of the Christian faith. You may have different beliefs about the second coming of Christ, or whether all the spiritual gifts are for today or not. One of you may enjoy an informal church service while the other likes a high church formal service, or one of you may be charismatic and the other not. It's important that your beliefs are important to you. You've made them something personal and significant for your life. There can still be spiritual intimacy within this diversity.[1]

Note
1. H. Norman Wright, *The Secrets of a Lasting Marriage* (Ventura, Calif.: Regal Books, 1995), pp. 153, 156.

How to Develop Spiritual Intimacy

MAKING YOUR EAR ATTENTIVE TO SKILLFUL AND
GODLY WISDOM, AND INCLINING AND DIRECTING YOUR
HEART AND MIND TO UNDERSTANDING [APPLYING ALL
YOUR POWERS TO THE QUEST FOR IT].

Proverbs 2:2 (Amp.)

FOR THE LORD GIVES SKILLFUL AND GODLY
WISDOM; FROM HIS MOUTH COME KNOWLEDGE
AND UNDERSTANDING.

Proverbs 2:6 (Amp.)

Some couples seem to be able to develop spiritual intimacy and others never do. What makes the difference? Spiritual intimacy has the opportunity to grow in a relationship that has a degree of stability. When the two of you experience trust, honesty, open communication, and dependability, you are more willing to risk being vulnerable spiritually. Creating this dimension will increase the stability factor as well.

We hear about mismatched couples when one is a Christian and one isn't. You can also have a mismatch when both are believers but one wants to grow and is growing, and the other doesn't and isn't!

A wonderful way to encourage spiritual intimacy is to share the history of your spiritual life. Many couples know where their spouses are currently, but very little of how they came to that place.

Use the following questions to discover more about your partner's faith:

1. What did your parents believe about God, Jesus, church, prayer, the Bible?
2. What was your definition of being spiritually alive?
3. Which parent did you see as being spiritually alive?

4. What specifically did each teach you directly and indirectly about spiritual matters?
5. Where did you first learn about God? About Jesus? About the Holy Spirit? What age?
6. What was your best experience in church as a child? As a teen?
7. What was your worst experience in church as a child? As a teen?
8. Describe your conversion experience. When? Who was involved? Where?
9. If possible, describe your baptism. What did it mean to you?
10. Which Sunday School teacher influenced you the most? In what way?
11. Which minister influenced you the most? In what way?
12. What questions did you have as a child/teen about your faith? Who gave you any answers?
13. Was there any camp or special meetings that affected you spiritually?
14. Did you read the Bible as a teen?
15. Did you memorize any Scripture as a child or teen? Do you remember any now?
16. As a child, if you could have asked God any questions, what would they have been?
17. As a teen, if you could have asked God any questions, what would they have been?
18. If you could ask God any questions now, what would they be?
19. What would have helped you more spiritually when you were growing up?
20. Did anyone disappoint you spiritually as a child? If so, how has that impacted you as an adult?
21. When you went through difficult times as a child or teen, how did that affect your faith?
22. What has been the greatest spiritual experience of your life?[1]

Note
1. H. Norman Wright, *The Secrets of a Lasting Marriage* (Ventura, Calif.: Regal Books, 1995), pp. 156-157.

Build Your Marriage on the Positives

AND BECOME USEFUL AND HELPFUL AND KIND TO ONE
ANOTHER, TENDERHEARTED (COMPASSIONATE, UNDER-
STANDING, LOVING-HEARTED), FORGIVING ONE ANOTHER
[READILY AND FREELY], AS GOD IN CHRIST FORGAVE YOU.

Ephesians 4:32 (Amp.)

Fact: Couples who have five times as many positives in their marriages as negatives have stable marriages. If that is the case, what can you do to make sure that positives abound in your marriage? Check the following ideas:

Shared Interests. It's important to share interest in your partner as a person, to discover what he/she has experienced during the day, to uncover any upset feelings. This can involve listening and looking at each other—without glancing at the TV or the paper on your lap. It can mean listening without attempting to fix a problem unless asked to do so.

Showing Affection. Being consistently affectionate—and not just at those times when one is interested in sex—is a highly valued positive response. Sometimes nothing is shared verbally. It can be sitting side by side and touching gently or moving close enough that you barely touch while you watch the sun dipping over a mountain with reddish clouds capturing your attention. It could be reaching out and holding hands in public. It can be doing something thoughtful, unrequested and noticed only by your partner.

Perhaps you're in the store and you see a favorite food your spouse enjoys and you buy it for him or her even if you hate it. Or you decide to stop at the store for an item and you call your spouse at home or at work to see if there's anything he or she wants or needs. You are "other" thinking rather than "self" thinking. You follow through with the scriptural teaching in Ephesians 4:32 (*NIV*), "Be kind and compassionate to one another."

SIXTEEN

An act of caring can be a phone call to ask if your partner has a prayer request. Acts of caring can mean remembering special dates and anniversaries without being reminded.

Showing Appreciation and Empathy. Another positive is being appreciative. This means going out of your way to notice all the little positive things your partner does and letting him or her know you appreciate them. It also means focusing on the positive experiences and dwelling upon those rather than the negative....Working toward agreement and appreciating the other's perspective is important. Compliments convey appreciation, but they need to be balanced between what persons do and who they are. Affirmations based on personal qualities are rare, but highly appreciated.

Showing genuine concern for your spouse when you notice he or she is upset builds unity and intimacy in a relationship. You may not be able to do anything, but sharing your desire to do so may be all that is necessary. When your partner shares a problem with you, don't relate a similar problem you once had, tell him what to do, crack jokes to cheer him up, or ask how he got into that problem in the first place. Instead, listen, put your arm around him, show that you understand, and let him know it's all right for him to feel and act the way he does.

I'm sure you've heard the word *empathy* time and time again.

Empathy includes rapport—knowing how your spouse would feel in most situations without him or her having to explain. You'll experience something together at the same time through the eyes of your partner.

The Lighter Side. Having a sense of humor and being able to laugh, joke, and have fun gives balance to the serious side of marriage. Some of what you laugh at will be private, and some will be shared with others. Having a sense of humor means you are able to laugh at yourself (even if it sometimes takes awhile!), and the two of you can laugh together. Sometimes the best memories are some of those hilarious incidents that happen even though your partner didn't think it was so funny at the time.[1]

Note
1. H. Norman Wright, *The Secrets of a Lasting Marriage* (Ventura, Calif.: Regal Books, 1995), pp. 52-55.

Create a Vision for Your Marriage

"AND IT WILL COME ABOUT AFTER THIS THAT
I WILL POUR OUT MY SPIRIT ON ALL MANKIND;
AND YOUR SONS AND DAUGHTERS WILL PROPHESY,
YOUR OLD MEN WILL DREAM DREAMS,
YOUR YOUNG MEN WILL SEE VISIONS."
Joel 2:28 (NASB)

Do you have a vision for your marriage? Perhaps the first question should be: Do you know what a vision is?

Vision can be thought of in many ways. Vision can be described as foresight, and the significance of possessing a keen awareness of current circumstances and possibilities, and the value of learning from the past.

Vision can also be described as seeing the invisible and making it visible. It is having a picture held in your mind of the way things could or should be in the days ahead.

Vision is also a portrait of conditions that don't yet exist. It is being able to focus more on the future than getting bogged down with the past or present. Vision is the process of creating a better future with God's empowerment and direction.[1]

The following are some other thoughts describing what vision means:

Vision is the dominant force that controls your life and influences the choices you make as a person and as a couple. It is what your thoughts lean toward when you are not focused on something else.

Vision can direct the kind of relationships and friendships you form. It is also what you pray about as you seek God's will.[2]

Vision is specific, detailed, customized, distinctive, and sometimes time related and measurable. In marriage, vision is a way of describing its activity and development. The vision you have for your marriage may be uniquely different from another person's. Having a vision for your marriage is having a realistic dream for what you, your spouse and your marriage can become when directed by God. We need to seek what God wants for us and our marriages because without His wisdom what we achieve may be out of His will. We need His wisdom because "The Lord knows the thoughts of man; he knows that they are futile" (Ps. 94:11).

Dr. Charles Stanley talks about vision for the Christian life:

> The Lord often shows us a general picture of what we are to do—and that broad overview tends to intimidate us and scare us. We need to realize that the Lord doesn't leave us with a giant goal or a great plan—He provides direction for all of the small steps that are necessary for getting to the big goal.
>
> Ask the Lord to show you the first step that you need toward the goal. Recognize that it will be only a step. Be patient with yourself and with God's working in you. Do what He shows you to do with all your strength, might, and talent. And then look for the second step that He leads you to take.
>
> The Lord doesn't catapult us into greatness: He grows us into spiritual maturity.
>
> He stretches us slowly so that we don't break.
>
> He expands our vision slowly so that we can take in all of the details of what He desires to accomplish.
>
> He causes us to grow slowly so that we stay balanced.
>
> The unfolding of God's plan for our lives is a process for the rest of your life.[3]

This wisdom applies to marriage as well. Talk about the vision you will develop for your marriage.

Notes
1. George Barna, *The Power of Vision* (Ventura, Calif.: Regal Books, 1992), pp. 28-29, adapted.
2. Phil Grand, "The Task Before Us," *European Bookseller* (May/June 1991): 48, adapted.
3. Charles Stanley, *The Source of My Strength* (Nashville: Thomas Nelson, 1994), p. 166.

Don't Let Criticism Creep into Your Marriage

SO DON'T CRITICIZE EACH OTHER ANY MORE. TRY
INSTEAD TO LIVE IN SUCH A WAY THAT YOU WILL
NEVER MAKE YOUR BROTHER STUMBLE BY LETTING HIM
SEE YOU DOING SOMETHING HE THINKS IS WRONG.

Romans 14:13 (TLB)

Guess what? You will complain about your partner from time to time. We all do. What else is new? Complaining is normal, but complaints can be voiced in a way that a spouse will hear them and not become defensive. For example, instead of focusing upon what annoys you, talk about what you would appreciate your spouse doing. Your partner is much more likely to hear you and consider your request if you show appreciation first, and then offer positive criticism.

Talking about what you don't like just reinforces the possibility of its continuing in greater intensity. The principle of pointing toward what you like also conveys to your partner your belief that he or she is capable of doing what you have requested. Doing this consistently, along with giving praise and appreciation when your spouse complies, will produce a change. Affirming and encouraging responses can literally change a person's life because we do want and need others to believe in us.

Criticism is the initial negative response that opens the door for the other destructive responses to follow. Criticism is different from complaining in that it attacks the other person's personality and character, usually by blaming. Most criticisms are overgeneralized ("You always...") and personally accusing (the word "you" is central). Most criticism comes in the form of blame, and the word "should" is usually included.

Criticism can be hidden, and is often camouflaged by joking. When confronted about it, a person will avoid responsibility by saying, "Hey, I was just joking." A passage in Proverbs says, "Like a madman who casts firebrands, arrows, and death, so is the man who deceives his neighbor and then says, Was I not joking?" (Prov. 26:18,19, *Amp.*).

Criticism is usually destructive, but it is common to hear critics say they are just trying to remold their partners into better persons by offering some "constructive" criticism. Too often, however, criticism does not construct; it demolishes. It does not nourish a relationship; it poisons. Often the presentation sounds like this: "There is one who speaks rashly like the thrusts of a sword" (Prov. 12:18, *NASB*). Criticism that is destructive accuses, tries to make the other feel guilty, intimidates and is often an outgrowth of personal resentment.

You have heard of "zingers," those lethal, verbal guided missiles. A zinger comes at you with a sharp point and a dull barb that catches the flesh as it penetrates. The power of these sharp, caustic statements is forceful when you realize that one zinger can undo 20 acts of kindness.[1]

A zinger has the power to render many positive acts meaningless. Once a zinger has landed, the effect is similar to a radioactive cloud that settles on an area of what used to be prime farmland. The land is so contaminated by the radioactivity that although seeds are scattered and plants are planted, they fail to take root. It takes decades for the contamination to dissipate. The kind acts of loving words following the placement of a zinger find a similar hostile soil. It may take hours before a receptive or positive response to your positive overtures is possible.

Another form of criticism is called "invalidation." It too is often the cause of marital distress. When invalidation is present in a marriage, it destroys the effect of validation, as well as the friendship relationship of marriage. Sometimes couples get along and maintain their relationships without sufficient validation, but they cannot handle continual invalidation. This is yet another example of one negative comment destroying 20 acts of kindness.[2]

Notes
1. Clifford Notarius and Howard Markman, *We Can Work It Out* (New York: G. P. Putnam's Sons, 1993), p. 28, adapted.
2. Ibid., pp. 123-124, adapted.

Agape Love in Your Marriage

JESUS REPLIED: "LOVE THE LORD YOUR GOD WITH
ALL YOUR HEART AND WITH ALL YOUR SOUL AND WITH
ALL YOUR MIND." THIS IS THE FIRST AND GREATEST
COMMANDMENT. AND THE SECOND IS LIKE IT:
"LOVE YOUR NEIGHBOR AS YOURSELF."

Matthew 22:37-39

AGAPE LOVE WILL LAST

Agape love manifests itself through several characteristics. First, it is an unconditional love. It is not based upon your spouse's performance, but upon your need to share this act of love with your spouse. If you don't, your spouse may live with the fear that you will limit your love if he or she does not meet your expectations.

Agape love is given in spite of how the other person behaves. It is a gift, rather than something that is earned. You are not obligated to love. This form of real love is an unconditional commitment to an imperfect person. It will require more of you than you ever realized; but that's what marriage is all about.

Agape love is also a transparent love. It is strong enough to allow your partner to get close to you and inside you. Transparency involves honesty, truth and sharing positive and negative feelings.

Agape love must be at the heart of a marriage. It is a self-giving love that keeps on going even when the other person is unlovable. This love will keep the other kinds of love alive. It involves being kind and sympathetic, thoughtful and sensitive to the needs of your loved one, even when you feel he or she doesn't deserve it.

Think about this:

Love means to commit yourself without guarantee, to give yourself completely in the hope that your love will produce love in the loved person. Love is an act of faith, and whoever is of little faith is also of little love. The perfect love would be one that gives all and expects nothing. It would, of course, be willing and delighted to take anything it was offered, the more the better. But it would ask for nothing. For if one expects nothing and asks nothing, she can never be deceived or disappointed. It is only when love demands that it brings on pain.[1]

AGAPE LOVE'S POWER

Agape love is a healing force. To demonstrate the power of this love, let's apply it to a critical area that affects marriage—irritability. Irritability is a carrier, and it keeps others at a distance if they know it is present within us. It is the launching pad for attack, lashing out, anger, sharp words, resentment and refusal of others' offers to love us.

Agape love is unique in that it causes us to seek to meet the needs of a mate rather than demanding that our own needs be reciprocated. Our irritability and frustrations diminish because we are seeking to fulfill another rather than pursuing our own needs and demanding their satisfaction.

Note
1. David L. Leuche, *The Relationship Manual* (Columbia, Md.: The Relationship Institute, 1981), p. 3, adapted.

You Are Unique—So Is Your Future Mate

IT IS FOR FREEDOM THAT CHRIST HAS SET US FREE.
STAND FIRM, THEN, AND DO NOT LET YOURSELVES BE
BURDENED AGAIN BY A YOKE OF SLAVERY.

Galatians 5:1

You are not a replica of your future mate. If you were, you probably wouldn't want to marry that person. You are not a replica of any other Christian either. Sometimes churches and well-meaning Christians try to remold us into revised editions of themselves or what they believe a Christian should be. If you fall prey to this fallacy, you will probably eventually be "under the law" in some legalistic structure. This is a new kind of slavery.

Today's verse (Gal. 5:1) states that we are not to allow slavery to happen to us. Unfortunately, this slavery happens in marriage. Each of you is drawn to your future partner by the person's uniqueness. After marriage, however, too many couples lose their appreciation of this uniqueness and see it as a pain in the neck. So they try to stifle and restrict this in a partner. This is slavery.

The way to be really free as a person and as a couple and to develop into all that God wants you to be, is to look to Him and His Word instead of looking to other people. Yes, others can give you some guidance and insight. So can your partner; but our basic source of study is God. Other people, like us, are imperfect. When we focus on them we often make wrong comparisons.

The Bible is full of comparison examples. Cain compared himself with Abel and killed him. Esau compared himself with Jacob, cared nothing about his birthright, and lost his inheritance. Saul compared himself to David and developed a mental breakdown. Those results aren't too encouraging, are they? Why look at others? That is slavery.

Think about the following two questions for a moment: What do you want your marriage to reflect? If the characteristics that come to mind are not present in other couples you know, are you willing to stand alone and be different? This could include letting your partner know that you are who you are and always will be. Your uniqueness will enhance your partner's life. Marriage is never to be a confinement, but an opportunity for each of you to be free and develop your potential to the utmost!

We have been set free by Christ. Although we have been set free, we can easily reattach the chains and handcuffs all by ourselves. Watch out that you don't sell yourself to some new slave master. The freedom you have was paid for, and it was costly. It cost God His Son. In setting you free, He was saying, "You are worth it. You are free. Follow Me alone."[1]

Note
1. H. Norman Wright, *Quiet Times for Couples* (Eugene, Oreg.: Harvest House Publishers, 1990), p. 355, adapted.

Who Will Be in Control?

IN THE TRUE SPIRIT OF HUMILITY (LOWLINESS OF
MIND) LET EACH REGARD THE OTHERS AS BETTER
THAN AND SUPERIOR TO HIMSELF.

Philippians 2:3 (Amp.)

Who's in charge here? Who's in control of this
project? These questions are asked thousands of
times each day, especially in business and indus-
try. However, they are rarely asked or even discussed in the marital relationship, and yet they
should be. The issue of control is one of the major
conflicts which can develop in a relationship. It
usually surfaces in some kind of power struggle
between partners.[1]

Which of you makes more decisions than the other, or is it
equal? Is one of you more dominant than the other? If so,
how will this affect your marriage?

Let's consider another factor about decision-making.
Which of you makes the decision more quickly?
What effect does this have? In any relationship it is
normal for one to be quicker and more decisive. This
doesn't mean that the faster person is any more
intelligent than the slower person.

The quicker spouse inserts his thoughts, plans
and procedures into the discussion first and has a
strong influence. He has the advantage and thus the
slower person tends to become even slower. He can't
keep pace or catch up.

It is better that there be a commitment by both
spouses to get involved in the overall decision-making process. We have to develop a "couple-pace" of
making decisions rather than maintaining our individual paces. The slow person can learn to go a bit

faster, and the faster one can learn to slow down. The point is to formulate our decisions together.[2]

If you've ever watched the interaction of puppies, you've probably noticed that power struggles are quite common. One puppy rises up to control and rule the rest of the pack. And if this puppy is taken from the litter first, another power struggle ensues until one puppy dominates. It's not very different from what we see occurring between humans. The desire to be in control and take charge of one's life has been evident in people since the Fall. Why is this? Why is the drive to be in control of everyone and everything so dominant in some people that their life is one pilgrimage after another for power?

Have you ever met a controller? Such a person must be right, must win, must be in charge, and must appear blameless. Ironically, gaining control doesn't satisfy the controller. He or she is usually unhappy, afraid of rejection, and unable to be intimate.

The pattern of controlling is counter to the scriptural pattern for marriage. [Not only that, when one person attempts to control a partner, it often kills the love in the relationship.] The attitude needed in marriage is reflected in Matthew 20:26-28; 23:11; Mark 9:35; 10:43-45; Luke 9:48; 22:26,27. Read these passages aloud. What do they say to you about what [your] husband and wife roles [will be] in marriage? How do these tie in to today's key verse...? All these passages reflect a way of life that Jesus says is better for individuals and couples. And He's right![3]

Notes
1. H. Norman Wright, *Quiet Times for Couples* (Eugene, Oreg.: Harvest House Publishers, 1990), p. 61.
2. H. Norman Wright, *So You're Getting Married* (Ventura, Calif.: Regal Books, 1985), pp. 127-128.
3. Wright, *Quiet Times for Couples*, p. 61.

The Gift of Listening

DEAR BROTHERS, DON'T EVER FORGET THAT IT IS BEST TO
LISTEN MUCH, SPEAK LITTLE, AND NOT BECOME ANGRY.

James 1:19 (TLB)

UNDERSTAND [THIS], MY BELOVED BRETHREN. LET EVERY
MAN BE QUICK TO HEAR [A READY LISTENER], SLOW TO
SPEAK, SLOW TO TAKE OFFENSE AND TO GET ANGRY.

James 1:19 (Amp.)

How well would your partner say you listen? You have
probably not asked him or her, have you? Would your partner say you are a ready listener, a reluctant listener or a selec-
tive listener? If you don't know, ask. While you are at it, ask,
"How could I be a better listener?" As he or she shares, keep
in mind this passage: "If you profit from constructive criticism you will be elected to the wise men's hall of fame. But
to reject criticism is to harm yourself and your own best
interests" (Prov. 15:31,32, *TLB*).

Have you ever said to your future partner, "Yes, I hear
you"? Probably. But hearing isn't listening. Consider this:

Hearing is basically to gain content or information for your
own purposes. Listening is caring for and being empathetic
toward the person who is talking. Hearing means that you are
concerned about what is going on inside you during the con-
versation. Listening means you are trying to understand the
feelings of your partner and are listening for the person's sake.

Think about this. Listening means that when your partner
is talking to you:

1. You are not thinking about what you are going to say
   when he or she stops talking. You are not busy formu-
   lating your response. You are concentrating on what is
   being said and are putting into practice Proverbs 18:13.
2. You are completely accepting what is being said without
   judging what he or she is saying or how he or she says it.

TWENTY-TWO

You may fail to hear the message if you are thinking that you don't like your partner's tone of voice or the words he or she is using. You may react on the spot to the tone and content and miss the meaning. Perhaps he or she hasn't said it in the best way; but why not listen and then come back later when both of you are calm and discuss the proper wording and tone of voice? Acceptance does not mean you have to agree with the content of what is said. Rather, it means you understand that what your partner is saying is something he or she feels.

3. You should be able to repeat what your partner has said and what you think he or she was feeling while speaking to you. Real listening implies an obvious interest in your partner's feelings and opinions and an attempt to understand them from his or her perspective.

You can learn to listen, for it is a skill to be learned. Your mind and ears can be taught to hear more clearly. Your eyes can be taught to see more clearly. But the reverse is also true. You can learn to hear with your eyes and see with your ears. Jesus said:

"Therefore I speak to them in parables; because while seeing they do not see, and while hearing they do not hear, nor do they understand. And in their case the prophecy of Isaiah is being fulfilled, which says, 'You will keep on hearing, but will not understand; and you will keep on seeing, but will not perceive; for the heart of this people has become dull, and with their ears they scarcely hear, and they have closed their eyes lest they should see with their eyes, and hear with their ears, and understand with their heart and return, and I should heal them'" (Matt. 13:13-15, *NASB*).

Let your ears hear and see. Let your eyes see and hear. One of the greatest gifts you will ever give your partner is listening with your undivided attention. Difficult? Perhaps. Possible to do? Definitely. Remember the one who listens to you no matter what and how you say it. God is our model for listening. We may be imperfect in our skills, but He isn't. Let Him help you become a better listener. Remember, unless there is listening, there is no communication.

Guidelines for Communication

A man finds joy in giving an apt reply—
and how good is a timely word!

Proverbs 15:23

Couples do a lot of talking, but is it really communication? Let's think about two things: What is communication, and what guidelines should we follow as we communicate?

Communication is the process of sharing yourself both verbally and nonverbally in such a way that the other person can understand and accept what you are sharing. Of course, it means you also have to attend with your ears and eyes so that the other person can communicate with you.

Communication is accomplished only when the other person receives the message you send, whether verbal or nonverbal. Communication can be effective, positive and constructive, or it can be ineffective, negative and destructive. While one [partner] may intend the message to be positive, the other...may receive it as a negative.

The Word of God is the most effective resource for learning to communicate. In it you will find a workable pattern for healthy relationships. Here are just a few guidelines it offers:

- "But speaking the truth in love, we are to grow up in all aspects into Him, who is the head, even Christ" (Eph. 4:15, *NASB*).
- "A man who refuses to admit his mistakes can never be successful. But if he confesses and forsakes them, he gets another chance" (Prov. 28:13, *TLB*).
- "For we all stumble in many ways. If any one does not stumble in what he says, he is a perfect man, able to bridle the whole body as well" (Jas. 3:2, *NASB*).

- "Let him who means to love life and see good days refrain his tongue from evil and his lips from speaking guile" (1 Pet. 3:10, *NASB*).
- "Some people like to make cutting remarks, but the words of the wise soothe and heal" (Prov. 12:18, *TLB*).
- "A wise man controls his temper. He knows that anger causes mistakes" (Prov. 14:29, *TLB*).
- "Gentle words cause life and health; griping brings discouragement....Everyone enjoys giving good advice, and how wonderful it is to be able to say the right thing at the right time!" (Prov. 15:4,23, *TLB*).
- "Timely advice is as lovely as golden apples in a silver basket" (Prov. 25:11, *TLB*).
- "A friendly discussion is as stimulating as the sparks that fly when iron strikes iron" (Prov. 27:17, *TLB*).
- "Pride leads to arguments; be humble, take advice and become wise" (Prov. 13:10, *TLB*).
- "Love forgets mistakes; nagging about them parts the best of friends" (Prov. 17:9, *TLB*).
- "Let all bitterness and wrath and anger and clamor and slander be put away from you, along with all malice. And be kind to one another, tender-hearted, forgiving each other, just as God in Christ also has forgiven you" (Eph. 4:31,32, *NASB*).[1]

So how do you remember these principles? It is simple; memorize each passage. Once each one is committed to memory, the Holy Spirit will bring them back to mind just when you need to be reminded the most. To encourage you in this process, you may want to begin with the following passage, which reinforces this point:

"Wherewithal shall a young man cleanse his way? by taking heed [thereto] according to thy word" (Ps 119:9, *KJV*).

Note
1. H. Norman Wright, *So You're Getting Married* (Ventura, Calif.: Regal Books, 1985), pp. 137-139.

Build a Romantic Marriage

[SO I WENT WITH HIM, AND WHEN WE WERE CLIMBING
THE ROCKY STEPS UP THE HILLSIDE, MY BELOVED SHEP-
HERD SAID TO ME] O MY DOVE, [WHILE YOU ARE HERE]
IN THE SECLUSION OF THE CLEFTS IN THE SOLID ROCK,
IN THE SHELTERED AND SECRET PLACE OF THE CLIFF,
LET ME SEE YOUR FACE, LET ME HEAR YOUR VOICE; FOR
YOUR VOICE IS SWEET, AND YOUR FACE IS LOVELY.

Song of Solomon 2:14 (Amp.)

Are you romantic? If so, great! If not, you can learn to be.
Your marriage will need it. You need it! But do you really
know what romance is?

A romantic relationship can include several important
ingredients. First, romance often includes the element of the
unexpected. The routines and tasks of our daily lives con-
sume most of our time and energy. An unexpected romantic
surprise can help break up the routine and monotony of the
day. Surprises also carry the message, "I'm thinking about
you. You're on my mind. I want your day to be different."

You may develop your own routine for creating special
romantic surprises. That is important. But beware: Anything
that is repeated month after month, year after year, or decade
after decade may become humdrum. Surprising your spouse
with dinner out at the same restaurant every payday may not
be as romantic after 20 years! Be sure to look for new restau-
rants, activities, and ways to say "I love you" that will keep
the excitement of the unexpected in your romancing.

A second element in a romantic relationship is called dating—something you now do and hopefully plan to continue.
Dating means selecting a specific time to be together and making plans for the event. Sometimes a couple may mutually plan
the activity or one person may be appointed to plan the date.

Most of the time romantic dating will be just for the two
of you and not a crowd! A few years from now when you're

out on a date, I would suggest not talking about work or the children. Rather, talk about yourselves. Make it a fun time. Laugh and enjoy each other and be a little crazy. When you go to a restaurant, let the host or hostess know that you and your spouse are there on a date.

Dates ought to center on an activity in which you can interact together. If you attend a movie or play, plan time before or after the show to eat and talk together.

Third, because romance is often emotional and nonrational, a romantic relationship sometimes includes the impractical. You may splurge on an outing or a gift, which you know you can't really afford, but the romantic value makes it worth scrimping in other areas to pay for it.

Impractical romantic happenings are moments to remember. And that is what romance is so often built upon—good memories. Store your hearts with romantic memories and they will carry you through the difficult times.

A fourth element in a romantic relationship is creativity. Discover what delights your partner and then make those delights happen in many different, creative ways. Even the way you express your love to your partner each day can be varied and innovative. If your spouse can predict what you will say, how you will respond and what kind of gift you will give on special occasions, you are in a romantic rut.

Fifth, romance involves daily acts of care, concern, love, speaking your partner's language, listening and giving each other your personal attention. Such acts convey a message of acceptance and thoughtfulness to your spouse. You see, romance begins in your mind and not in your glands. Too many people, especially men, tend to let their physical drives take the lead in romance all the time. Rather, a thoughtful, caring attitude will create romance even when your glands are stuck in neutral.

Sixth, romance involves commitment. Every day of our lives as couples is marked by highs and lows, joys and disappointments. Romantic feelings will ebb and flow. If commitment to each other is at the heart of the marriage relationship, however, romance will thrive. Mutual commitment creates a mutual love response, and commitment is first an exercise of the will based on an attitude of heart.

TWENTY-FIVE

When You're Angry...

HE WHO IS SLOW TO ANGER IS BETTER THAN
THE MIGHTY, AND HE WHO RULES HIS [OWN]
SPIRIT THAN HE WHO TAKES A CITY.

Proverbs 16:32 (Amp.)

An angry wife. An angry husband. An angry marriage! Is it common? Most of the anger we experience in life concerns relationships, so why should the marriage relationship be excluded? It isn't. Marriage probably generates in couples more anger than they will experience in any other relationship. Perhaps you have already experienced this in your engagement. When two people live together constantly with vulnerability and closeness, the potential for hurt and misunderstanding is enormous. Learning to function in harmony without one overriding the other takes delicate skill and extended practice.

Anger and love can exist in the same relationship. When anger is always smoldering, however, it tends to diminish the quality of love. In time, resentment gains a foothold. Resentment is an eroding disease that feeds on lingering anger for its lifeblood. Resentment eats away at the relationship until the love is dead. Worse, if resentment continues, it eventually can produce hate—and hate separates. It drives the other person away. No couple planning to be married wants this to happen.

Anger is a normal part of close relationships. Whenever two people begin a relationship, part of what attracts them are their similarities and another part of what attracts them are their differences. Opposites do attract, but not for long. It does not take much time for differences to lead to disagreements. Disagreements may involve the emotions of fear, hurt and frustration.

- Fear that our relationship is threatened and that we will never be understood.
- Hurt about what has been said to us and about us, or how it has been said.

- Frustration that we have had a similar disagreement before and this is the same song, twenty-second verse.

Disagreements often involve anger and lead to conflict. At that point we have a choice. We can choose to spend our anger-energy by dumping on our spouse, showing our victim where, once again, he or she is clearly wrong and we are right. We can also choose to throw up our hands in futility and stomp out of the room. By that act we communicate one of two things. Either the other person is not worth taking the time to work out the issue, or communication between the two of us is impossible. Both choices lead to feelings of hopelessness and helplessness and set us up for more failure in the future.

We can, however, choose another option. We can acknowledge our fear, hurt or frustration and choose to invest our anger-energy by seizing this opportunity to better understand our loved one. One of the most practical ways is to remember that love "bears all things, believes all things, hopes all things, endures all things" (1 Cor. 13:7, *NKJV*), and to develop the habit of working through our differences. This takes time and involves listening, asking questions, listening, asking more questions, and finally reaching understanding.

Do not be quick in spirit to be angry or vexed, for anger and vexation lodge in the bosom of fools (Eccles. 7:9, *Amp.*).

The beginning of strife is as when water first trickles [from a crack in a dam]; therefore stop contention before it becomes worse and quarreling breaks out (Prov. 17:14, *Amp.*).

Good sense makes man restrain his anger, and it is his glory to overlook a transgression or an offense (Prov. 19:11, *Amp.*).

Cease from anger and forsake wrath; fret not yourself—it tends only to evil-doing (Ps. 37:8, *Amp.*).

When angry, do not sin; do not ever let your wrath (your exasperation, your fury or indignation) last until the sun goes down (Eph. 4:26, *Amp.*).[1]

Note
1. Gary J. Oliver and H. Norman Wright, *When Anger Hits Home* (Chicago: Moody Press, 1992), pp. 87-159, adapted.

Can You Change Your Partner?

THEREFORE LET US STOP PASSING JUDGMENT ON ONE
ANOTHER. INSTEAD, MAKE UP YOUR MIND NOT TO PUT ANY
STUMBLING BLOCK OR OBSTACLE IN YOUR BROTHER'S WAY.

Romans 14:13

Each of you has a calling in marriage. It is to be an encourager rather than a critic, a forgiver rather than a collector of hurts, an enabler rather than a reformer. By doing these things you help your partner become all that it is possible for him or her to become. You are called to make things easy or possible.

Too often people discover that marriage stifles and limits rather than frees them to become all they can be. Often this is because one spouse adopts the role of critical reformer. Reformers try to get their partners to meet their own standards or become replicas of themselves. Insecure people want their mates' behaviors, beliefs and attitudes to be just like their own, and they are threatened by any real or supposed differences. This is not a healthy request for change.

Consider the following:

"Some spouses seem to have an almost irresistible urge to reform or improve their partners in some respect. It's constant; there's never any satisfaction. A wife may want to make her husband more socially acceptable, or to get him to take more responsibility around the house. A husband wants his wife to be a better housekeeper, or to be more organized. Sometimes even the tiniest habits seem to require corrective action; the way one dresses, the way one walks, the way one squeezes a tube of toothpaste.

"All of us need to change and grow in hundreds of different ways. But it's a problem when a husband or wife appoints himself or herself a Committee of One to see that the necessary change is enacted, and in doing so says, "You must change; I can't really accept you as you are until you get busy and do it." The result is that grace is smothered and all genuine desire for love-motivated change is undercut."[1]

TWENTY-SIX

There's the difference! A demand confines; a request gives freedom. Do you know how to request rather than demand?

Years ago I discovered a wise quote:

"We try to change people to conform to our ideas of how they should be. So does God. But there the similarity ends. The way in which we try to get other people to conform is far different than the way in which God works with us. Our ideas of what the other person should do or how he should act may be an improvement or an imprisonment. We may be setting the other person free of behavior patterns that are restricting his development, or we may be simply chaining him up in another behavioral bondage. The changes God works in us are always freeing, freeing to become that which he has created us to be."[2]

Whatever change you will seek needs to be advantageous for both you and your partner, as well as for the relationship. It is not our responsibility to take on the job of reformer. The Holy Spirit can do that much better than we can. Our task is to request changes of our spouses and to provide an atmosphere of acceptance and patience that allows God freedom to work. Then we must learn to trust God to do the work.

Satisfying marriages have a common ingredient—mutual education. Mutual education means that both of you must become skilled teachers as well as receptive learners. The reason for this is to develop a greater degree of compatibility. If you neglect this education process, your relationship could be in jeopardy.

Mutual education is a gentle process. It involves positive modeling of the desired attitudes or behavior, gentle prodding, sensitive reminders, encouragement, believing your spouse can succeed and not blaming or rebuking. It focuses on the positive, and you want to manage that change so the end result is positive.[3] I am sure that is what you want too.

Notes
1. Joseph Cooke, *Free for the Taking* (Grand Rapids: Fleming H. Revell, 1975), p. 127.
2. James Fairfield, *When You Don't Agree* (Scottdale, Pa.; Herald Press, 1977), p. 195.
3. Jeanette C. Lauer and Robert H. Lauer, *Till Death Do Us Part* (New York: Harrington Park Press, 1986), pp. 153-154, adapted.

Are You Marrying an Alien?

FINALLY, BRETHREN, FAREWELL (REJOICE)! BE
STRENGTHENED (PERFECTED, COMPLETED, MADE WHAT
YOU OUGHT TO BE); BE ENCOURAGED AND CONSOLED AND
COMFORTED; BE OF THE SAME [AGREEABLE] MIND ONE
WITH ANOTHER; LIVE IN PEACE, AND [THEN] THE GOD OF
LOVE [WHO IS THE SOURCE OF AFFECTION, GOODWILL,
LOVE, AND BENEVOLENCE TOWARD MEN] AND THE
AUTHOR AND PROMOTER OF PEACE WILL BE WITH YOU.

2 Corinthians 13:11 (Amp.)

AND LET THE PEACE OF CHRIST RULE IN YOUR HEARTS,
TO WHICH INDEED YOU WERE CALLED IN ONE BODY;
AND BE THANKFUL.

Colossians 3:15 (NASB)

Differences. How do you learn to adjust to the differences in your partner without losing who you are? How do you learn to appreciate another person's uniqueness? How can you learn to live with this person who is so, so different from you? As one wife said, "It's not just that I married an alien from another planet! Did I join the cast of *Star Trek* or marry someone left over from the film series *Star Wars*? Help!"

People ask the question, "Should you marry someone who is your opposite or someone who is similar?"

The answer is yes—yes to both. Some similarities as well as some opposites will be present, and you have to learn to adjust to both. Think of it like this:

> We marry for our similarities. We stay together for our differences. Similarities satiate, differences attract. Differences are rarely the cause of conflict in marriage. The problems arise from our similarities. Differences are the occasion, similarities are the cause.
>
> The differences may serve as the triggering event,

as the issue for debate or the beef for our hassle, but it's the similarities that create the conflict between us.

The very same differences that initially drew us together, later press us apart and still later may draw us near again. Differences first attract, then irritate, then frustrate, then illuminate and finally may unite us. Those traits that intrigue in courtship, amuse in early marriage begin to chafe in time and infuriate in the conflicts of middle marriage; but maturation begins to change their meaning and the uniqueness of the other person becomes prized, even in the very differences that were primary irritants.[1]

Differences abound in any marriage. Generally, they can be divided into two types. The first includes those that can't be helped, such as age, race, looks, home, and cultural background. Your personal body metabolism will affect where you want the temperature in the home, whether you wake up bright and eager, ready to face the day, or whether you need an hour to get both eyes focusing. These differences cannot be changed.

But the other type of difference involves those that can be changed. These can include personal habits in the bathroom or at the dinner table, whether you like to get up early and your spouse enjoys sleeping late, or whether one likes going out three nights a week and the other prefers watching television at home. I'm amazed at how small learned behaviors, such as having the bed covers tucked in rather than having them loose or eating a TV dinner rather than a four-course dinner on a tablecloth, become such major issues in marriage.[2]

Have you listed your differences and your similarities? If not, this may be a good time to do so. The sooner you understand them, the sooner you can learn to become compatible.

Notes
1. David Augsburger, *Sustaining Love* (Ventura, Calif.: Regal Books, 1988), p. 40.
2. H. Norman Wright, *The Secrets of a Lasting Marriage* (Ventura, Calif.: Regal Books, 1995), p. 119.

Are You Marrying the Right Person?

LIVING AS BECOMES YOU WITH COMPLETE LOWLINESS
OF MIND (HUMILITY) AND MEEKNESS (UNSELFISHNESS,
GENTLENESS, MILDNESS), WITH PATIENCE, BEARING
WITH ONE ANOTHER AND MAKING ALLOWANCES
BECAUSE YOU LOVE ONE ANOTHER.

Ephesians 4:2 (Amp.)

Sometimes people question if they are marrying the right person. This is especially true in the first couple of years when a partner's differences unfold. The following discovery process of differences is typical.

You are vaguely aware of the differences when you first marry. At the time, you certainly wouldn't say that your partner is different—more likely "unique." After a while, however, it is different. At first you may try to accommodate. You tolerate, overlook or deny differences to avoid conflict.

Then you eliminate, or try to purge, the differences in one another by demanding, pressuring or manipulating.

Then you start to appreciate because you discover the differences are necessary and indispensable. They are essential. Because of this you are able to celebrate them. You delight in them. You welcome them. You encourage their growth.[1]

Couples discover through this process that they didn't marry the wrong person. Think about this:

In reality, we marry the right person—far more right than we can know. In a mysterious, intuitive, perhaps instinctive fashion we are drawn by both similarities and differences, by needs and anxieties, by dreams and fears to choose our complement, our reflection in another.

We always marry the right person, and the discovery of that rightness moves us into the third marriage within a marriage. We at last begin to appreciate what we had sought to eliminate.

As we each discover that we knew more than we knew when we chose whom we chose, appreciation begins to break into a gentle flame. In appreciation, we discover that people who marry each other *reflect* each other....The two express their self-image and self-valuation in the person selected.

People who marry each other *complete* each other in a puzzling yet pronounced way. The missing is supplied, the imbalanced is brought into equilibrium, the dormant is enriched by what is dominant in the other.[2]

Well, what do you do now? Study your partner. Study yourself. Decide how you could respond differently. Expand your knowledge of gender differences, personality differences, and how to speak in a language that your partner understands.

You may be surprised and amazed by what you discover. And you know what? It will be worth the minimal amount of time it will take to bring a new and better level of harmony and adjustment to your marriage. It's an ingredient for a lasting marriage. It will help you celebrate your differences.

The adventure of marriage is discovering who your partner really is. The excitement is in finding out who your partner will become.[3]

Notes
1. David Augsburger, *Sustaining Love* (Ventura, Calif.: Regal Books, 1988), p. 38, adapted.
2. Ibid., pp. 54, 56.
3. H. Norman Wright, *The Secrets of a Lasting Marriage* (Ventura, Calif.: Regal Books, 1995), pp. 128-129.

Your Partner
Is a Gift

EVERY GOOD AND PERFECT GIFT IS FROM ABOVE, COMING
DOWN FROM THE FATHER OF THE HEAVENLY LIGHTS,
WHO DOES NOT CHANGE LIKE SHIFTING SHADOWS.

James 1:17

Marriage is a gift. You may be the finest gift your partner has ever received! Your partner may be the finest gift you have received.

A gift is an item that is selected with care and consideration. Its purpose is to bring delight and fulfillment to another, an expression of deep feeling on the part of the giver.

Think of the care and effort you put into selecting a gift. You wonder what the recipient would enjoy. What will bring him or her delight? What will bring happiness? What will make his or her day bright and cheery? What will show the person the extent of your feeling for him or her and how much the person means to you?

Because you want this gift to be special and meaningful, you spend time thinking about what gift to select. Then you begin the search through various stores and shops, considering and rejecting several items until the right one beckons to you and you make the selection. You invest time wrapping the gift. You think of how best to present it to the person so his or her delight and pleasure will be heightened.

Excitement and a challenge is involved in selecting and presenting a special gift. You not only have given the object, but you also have given your time and energy. Gifts that are often appreciated the most are not those that are the most expensive, but those that reflect the investment of yourself in considering the desires and wants of the other person. The way you present it and your sacrifice also make a gift special.

You are a gift to your partner. If you consider yourself a gift, how will you live so your partner believes he or she has been given a special gift? Will you invest your time, thought and energy in your spouse? Will your partner experience delight, fulfillment and a feeling of being special? How can you, as a gift, be used in the life of your spouse to lift his or her spirits and outlook on life?

On the receiving end of the gift, how do you react when you receive a special gift that brings you delight? Think of your childhood years. What was the most exciting or special gift you ever received? Can you remember your thoughts and feelings as you received that gift? How did you treat that gift? Did you take special care of it and protect it from harm and loss? Perhaps you gave the gift a special place of prominence and were carefully possessive of it.

If your spouse is a special gift to you, how will you treat this gift? Will you be careful to give your partner the finest care, attention, protection and place of prominence in your life? Will your partner feel as though he or she really is a gift to you?

A gift is given as an expression of our love. It is not based on whether the recipient deserves it or not. Our giving of a gift is actually an act of grace.

Why not talk about how you can be a gift to one another?

Rejoice in Your Sexuality

FOR THIS REASON A MAN WILL LEAVE HIS FATHER AND
MOTHER AND BE UNITED TO HIS WIFE, AND THEY WILL
BECOME ONE FLESH. THE MAN AND HIS WIFE WERE
BOTH NAKED, AND THEY FELT NO SHAME.

Genesis 2:24,25

Let's talk about sex—finally. We *are* sexual beings. God created us this way. It is His idea and His gift to us.

You and your future partner have talked about sex, or you should have by now. But have you talked with God about it in prayer? If not, the following prayer expresses what many couples feel and struggle with today. Perhaps this reflects where you are, too.

> Lord, it's hard to know what sex really is—Is it some demon put here to torment me? Or some delicious seducer from reality? It is neither of these, Lord.
> I know what sex is—
> It is body and spirit,
> It is passion and tenderness,
> It is strong embrace and gentle hand-holding, It is open nakedness and hidden mystery, It is joyful tears in honeymoon faces at a golden wedding anniversary.
> Sex is a quiet look across the room, a love note on a pillow, a rose laid on a breakfast plate, laughter in the night. Sex is life—not all of life—but wrapped up in the meaning of life. Sex is your good gift, O God, To enrich life, To continue the race, To communicate, To show me who I am, To reveal my mate, To cleanse through "one flesh."
> Lord, some people say sex and religion don't mix; But your Word says sex is good. Help me to keep it good in my life. Help me to be open about sex. And still protect its mystery. Help me to see that sex is nei-

ther demon nor deity. Help me not to climb into a fantasy world of imaginary sexual partners; keep me in the real world to love the people you have created.

Teach me that my soul does not have to frown at sex for me to be a Christian. It's hard for many people to say, "Thank God for sex!" Because for them sex is more a problem than a gift. They need to know that sex and gospel can be linked together again. They need to hear the good news about sex. Show me how I can help them.

Thank you Lord, for making me a sexual being. Thank you for showing me how to treat others with trust and love. Thank you for letting me talk to you about sex. Thank you that I feel free to say: "Thank God for sex!"[1]

Note
1. Harry Hollis Jr., *Thank God for Sex* (Nashville: Broadman & Holman, 1975), pp. 11-12.

God's Word and Sex

DRINK WATER FROM YOUR OWN CISTERN, RUNNING
WATER FROM YOUR OWN WELL. SHOULD YOUR SPRINGS
OVERFLOW IN THE STREETS, YOUR STREAMS OF WATER
IN THE PUBLIC SQUARES? LET THEM BE YOURS ALONE,
NEVER TO BE SHARED WITH STRANGERS. MAY YOUR
FOUNTAIN BE BLESSED, AND MAY YOU REJOICE IN THE
WIFE OF YOUR YOUTH. A LOVING DOE, A GRACEFUL
DEER—MAY HER BREASTS SATISFY YOU ALWAYS, MAY
YOU EVER BE CAPTIVATED BY HER LOVE.

Proverbs 5:15-19

The Bible often uses water as a powerful and fitting metaphor for cleansing, healing and rejuvenating. It contains beautiful images such as "streams in the desert," "water of life" and "beside the still waters." What a tremendous portrayal of the dynamic nature of lovemaking to compare it to a cistern, a well, a stream and a fountain of water. It imitates a cool, refreshing drink from your own safe supply.

In one way, your sex life will resemble a cistern in which you will store many amorous memories and a sexy repertoire of arousing activities. You will be able to dip into it again and again in your fantasy life and lovemaking for excitement and fun. In another way, making love is like a stream or spring of water. Sex in marriage has an ever-changing, renewing quality to it. As the ancient Greek philosopher Heraclitus gazed into the river and realized life was a dynamic process that never stayed the same, so you can anticipate infinite variety and newness in making love.

A routine sex life is not God's design. You can make love four times a week for the next 50 years and still never plumb the surprising depths of this mysterious sexual "stream" of becoming one flesh.

The words "rejoice," "satisfy" and "captivated" in the Proverbs passage are positive expressions. Pleasure and fun are an intended part of making love. It is important for spouses to enjoy playing together. You can rejoice with the mate of your youth. Your creativity, imagination and love can allow you to remain ever enthralled sexually with the lover of your youth. You can be ever satisfied and captivated for the life of your marriage.

Don't let your sexual relationship become routine or stagnant. Be creative.

Sex is an erotic celebration! *Eros*, the Greek word for sexual love, includes the ideas of fusion, passion, attraction and bonding. Erotic love is becoming lost in someone's eyes. Erotic love is mental imagery, anticipation, playfulness, ambiance and lovers physically enjoying each other.

The Song of Solomon contains many beautiful images of erotic love:

> Let him kiss me with the kisses of his mouth—For your love is better than wine (1:2, *NKJV*).
>
> My lover is mine and I am his; he browses among the lilies (2:16).
>
> Your two breasts are like two fawns,... Your plants are an orchard of pomegranates with choice fruits,... You are a garden fountain, a well of flowing water... Let my lover come into his garden and taste its choice fruits (4:5,13,15,16).
>
> I have become...like one bringing contentment. But my own vineyard is mine to give (8:10,12).

You may want to read the Song of Solomon out loud to one another on your honeymoon. On second thought, read it frequently during the year. It will help you celebrate God's gift.[1]

Note

1. Douglas F. Rosenau, *A Celebration of Sex* (Nashville: Thomas Nelson, 1994), pp. 21-22, adapted.

Be a Cheerleader

IF YOU LOVE SOMEONE YOU WILL BE LOYAL TO HIM
NO MATTER WHAT THE COST. YOU WILL ALWAYS
BELIEVE IN HIM, ALWAYS EXPECT THE BEST OF HIM,
AND ALWAYS STAND YOUR GROUND IN DEFENDING HIM.

1 Corinthians 13:7 (TLB)

Has anyone told you that one of your roles as a spouse will be a cheerleader for your partner? That's right, a cheerleader. Do you know what a cheerleader is? Perhaps in your school days you or your partner were a cheerleader for your school. Now your team will be made up of one person—your partner; and that person needs you to cheer him or her on in life! We all need someone to believe in us and cheer for us, especially when things are not going well.

During the 1992 Winter Olympics, a former Olympic skater named Scott Hamilton served as one of the commentators for the ice-skating events. At one point, Hamilton shared about his special relationship with his mother who had died just prior to his winning an Olympic gold medal.

"The first time I skated in the U.S. Nationals, I fell five times. My mother gave me a big hug and said, 'It's only your first national. It's no big deal.' My mother always let me be me. Three years later I won my first National. She never said, 'You can do better,' or 'Shape up.' She just encouraged me." This mother knew how to edify her son.

Edifying is often used in the New Testament to refer to building up another person. Three examples of edifying are expressed in the following verses: (1) giving personal encouragement, (2) providing inner strength and (3) establishing peace and harmony between people.

> So let us then definitely aim for and eagerly pursue what makes for harmony and for mutual upbuilding (edification and development) of one another (Rom. 14:19, *Amp.*).

Let each one of us make it a practice to please (make happy) his neighbor for his good and for his true welfare, to edify him [to strengthen him and build him up spiritually] (Rom. 15:2, *Amp.*).

Therefore encourage one another and build each other up, just as in fact you are doing (1 Thess. 5:11).

First Corinthians 8:1 sums up the matter of edifying: "Love builds up."

Anne Morrow Lindbergh experienced a deep personal tragedy. Her husband, famous aviator Charles Lindbergh, was always in the limelight. As a result of the kidnapping and death of their son, Mrs. Lindbergh also became a public figure.[1] The following are her thoughts about being loved and believed in:

> To be deeply in love, of course, is a great liberating force and the most common experience that frees.... Ideally, both members of a couple in love free each other to new and different worlds. I was no exception to the general rule. The sheer fact of finding myself loved was unbelievable and changed my world, my feelings about life and myself. I was given confidence, strength, and almost a new character.[2]

Have you learned to release your partner to discover his or her hidden potential that has yet to emerge? Your partner belongs to the Lord, and He wants the best for both of you.

Perhaps your partner needs a little more cheering on from you. Perhaps he or she needs a phone call or a personal note from you: Go for it; you can do it. I'm here for you; I believe in you. Give it a try; I'm praying for you. These are the kinds of words that cheer a person on. Make cheerleading a consistent pattern in your relationship now and in marriage. It may help to ask, "How can I be a better cheerleader for you?"[3]

Notes
1. Charles R. Swindoll, *Growing Strong in the Seasons of Life* (Portland, Oreg.: Multnomah Press, 1983), adapted from pp. 169, 170.
2. Ibid., p. 170.
3. H. Norman Wright, *Quiet Times for Couples* (Eugene, Oreg.: Harvest House Publishers, 1990), p. 36, adapted.

God's Encouragement

DO NOTHING OUT OF SELFISH AMBITION OR
VAIN CONCEIT, BUT IN HUMILITY CONSIDER
OTHERS BETTER THAN YOURSELVES.

Philippians 2:3

A vital step to the growth of any marriage is learning to reflect the Word of God as it relates to marriage. Some couples discuss the meaning of one particular passage of Scripture. Then they both describe how they will put this passage into practice during the coming week. The following Scripture passages can be used for this purpose in your marriage:

- Love one another (John 13:34).
- Carry each other's burdens (Gal 6:2).
- Bearing with one another in love (Eph. 4:2).
- Serve one another (Gal. 5:13).
- Submit to one another (Eph. 5:21).
- In humility consider others better than yourselves (Phil. 2:3).
- Be kind and compassionate to one another (Eph. 4:32).
- Honor one another (Rom. 12:10).
- Encourage one another (1 Thess. 5:11a).
- Build each other up (1 Thess. 5:11b).
- Accept one another (Rom. 15:7).
- Instruct one another (Rom. 15:14).
- Have equal concern for each other (1 Cor. 12:25).
- Pray for each other (Jas. 5:16).

Time and time again, the Word of God admonishes us to behave in a positive and encouraging way.

And become useful and helpful and kind to one another, tenderhearted (compassionate, understanding, loving-hearted), forgiving one another [readily and freely], as God in Christ forgave you (Eph. 4:32, *Amp.*).

THIRTY-THREE

Clothe yourselves therefore, as God's own chosen ones (His own picked representatives), [who are] purified and holy and well-beloved [by God Himself, by putting on behavior marked by] tender-hearted pity and mercy, kind feeling, a lowly opinion of yourselves, gentle ways, [and] patience [which is tireless and long-suffering, and has the power to endure whatever comes, with good temper]. Be gentle and forbearing with one another and, if one has a difference (a grievance or complaint) against another, readily pardoning each other; even as the Lord has [freely] forgiven you, so must you also [forgive] (Col. 3:12,13, *Amp.*).

I recently read a news story about a small airplane that had been lost. The pilot's wife called the authorities to tell them her husband had gone flying the day before and had never returned. Their first question was, "Did he file a flight plan?" Because the pilot had not filed a flight plan, the rescuers were unable to help. They had no way to determine where this pilot was planning to fly. They couldn't begin to devise a search and rescue plan.

Pilots usually file a flight plan to help them determine course settings and let others know their intended destination. Marriage is no different. Filing a flight plan removes an added element of risk from the marital journey. True, you might still run into occasional turbulence. Having no automatic pilot, you might begin to drift off course if you don't keep your eyes on the compass and your hands on the controls at all times.

Can you envision using the previous Scriptures as the flight plan and guiding compass for attitudes and behavior within your family? Practicing God's words of encouragement offers another important way to actively build your marriage.

Who Is in Charge?

SO THAT WITH ONE HEART AND MOUTH YOU
MAY GLORIFY THE GOD AND FATHER OF OUR
LORD JESUS CHRIST.

Romans 15:6

Power! Control! More power! More control! Nations want power, corporations strive for power, politicians want power, interest groups want power. It seems that everyone has this determined drive to gain more power and control. Marriages are not immune from this unquenchable thirst. Power struggles are one of the biggest perpetrators of conflict in marriage. Couples argue about many issues, but underlying many of them is a power struggle.

Dictionaries provide a variety of definitions for the word "power." One is the possession of control, authority or influence over others. The *Oxford English Dictionary* defines authority as "power or right to enforce obedience...the right to command or give an ultimate decision." Therefore, in a marital relationship when one partner has the bulk of the power or authority, he or she has most of the control and makes most of the decisions! The person on the other side then feels inferior, dependent, abused, neglected and downtrodden and has attitudes of dejection, anger and resentment.

Years ago we raised shelties in our home. A sheltie looks like a miniature collie and is an intelligent dog—until it gets into a tug-of-war with another puppy. They both sit there and pull and pull on the towel and neither of them gets anywhere. They wear themselves out pulling, trying to get the towel away from the other puppy. If they were really smart, they might figure out that what they are doing isn't working. If one sheltie would let up on one end of the towel, it would probably knock the other puppy off balance, dislodge the towel and then the smart puppy could run away with it all to itself.

When Jesus Christ is Lord of you, your partner and your

marriage, several good things will happen to enhance and enrich your marriage. Consider these possibilities:

Jesus as Lord of your marriage relieves each of you of the burden of "lording it over" the other. It is part of our fallen nature to want to control each other rather than sacrificially to serve one another. When we submit ourselves to the Lord Jesus Christ, however, competition turns into loving empathy.

Enrolling ourselves under the lordship of Jesus Christ turns each of us into both the student and the teacher of the other. Jesus opens our hearts to each other and enables us to learn from each other.

A husband and wife with Jesus as Lord have in Him a higher authority than themselves, and thus they do not insist on "playing God" in the lives of their children. When we feel we are the final authority over our children, we lose our capacity to learn from them.

Husbands and wives with Jesus as Lord have in Him a leader in times of major decision-making. When we turn to the Lord Jesus Christ and open our consciences to His Spirit's leading, some new events, remembrances, and forgotten facts will come to us. A whole new pattern will emerge.

When Jesus is Lord of our marriages, He keeps us from idolizing each other and expecting each other to be perfect. He enables us to affirm each other's humanness, and to bear the burdens of each other's faults, thus fulfilling the law of Christ.[1]

What can you say to your partner after reading this?

Note

1. Wayne Oates, "Husbands and Wives with Jesus as Lord," in Howard and Jeanne Hendricks, eds., *Husbands and Wives* (Wheaton, Ill.: Victor Books, 1988), pp. 157-159.

What Will You Collect?

GET RID OF ALL BITTERNESS, RAGE AND ANGER, BRAWL-
ING AND SLANDER, ALONG WITH EVERY FORM OF MALICE.
BE KIND AND COMPASSIONATE TO ONE ANOTHER, FORGIV-
ING EACH OTHER, JUST AS IN CHRIST GOD FORGAVE YOU.

Ephesians 4:31,32

Have you ever been to the Grand Tetons—those majestic mountains rising thousands of feet from the floor of Jackson Hole, their ragged terrain and year-round glacial patches looking something like the Swiss Alps? During the past 26 years Joyce and I have been there 20 times. It is our favorite place to be refreshed and enjoy a dramatic reminder of God's handiwork. We have fished, hiked many trails and areas where no trails existed, floated the Snake River and waded the various streams in search of beautiful cutthroat trout.

One morning Joyce and I put on our daypacks and started walking up the trail to Bradley Lake. We walked the two miles up the sloping paths and when we arrived we were fresh and rested. We had limited the number of items we carried with us so the weight of our packs wouldn't become a wearisome burden. We wanted to walk at a brisk pace, enjoy the surroundings and have energy when we arrived.

Arriving about nine in the morning, we left the trail and walked through the wet grass into the last small stand of trees. We emerged from the woods to find ourselves on level ground adjoining the lake. From there we proceeded to the sandbar. Taking off our daypacks and coats, we put the finishing touches on our fishing equipment and went to work. I let the line drift into the current of the small stream at the inlet of the lake; the natural force and pull of the stream took our line. A few seconds later a violent pull vibrated up the length of the pole. The battle was on. Joyce was as excited as I was. A minute later we saw a 17-inch reddish brown cutthroat trout coming through the clear water.

Landing that first fish was just the start of a delightful

morning for the two of us. We hiked through forest and meadows, climbed over downed trees, scrambled over rough shorelines and waded through shallow water. Along the way we saw many rocks and pieces of driftwood that we would have liked to take back with us. We began picking up some unusual rocks and pieces of wood. But as we continued we realized we were becoming absorbed with collecting. I had limited how far we would be able to explore and travel. Our daypacks would not be able to contain all we were thinking of collecting. We also thought about how exhausted we would be carrying all these items back to our car. We than made a wise decision. We put all the items back where we found them. They belonged there and not with us.

Our hike back around the lake was pleasant and not a burden. Had we taken what we thought we needed, our attention would have been upon the weight of what we had collected as it rested more and more heavily upon our shoulders. It would have distracted us from the beauty of the clear skies, Indian paintbrush and columbine, and the gentle wind whispering through the pine and aspen trees. It was a day to remember.

Many individuals and couples carry a weight around with them unnecessarily. This keeps them from experiencing life to its fullest. Some are collectors. They collect excess emotional baggage that acts as an anchor hindering both progress and direction.

Some people collect garbage. Some collect stamps. Some collect records and fine art. And some collect hurts!

Many of the hurts we experience we never deserved. During conflict between married partners—which you will have—words are exchanged that penetrate and sometimes change the partner. Some words are like arrows: they enter the victim and when the shaft of the arrow is pulled free, the jagged point remains to fester and keep the hurt alive. If you have already been hurt by your partner for one reason or another, I am sure you have wished you could reach back to that painful encounter and cut it out of your life.

The good news for the past and the future is that you *can* cut the pain from your life. How? It is called God's grace. He will help you let loose of those painful hurts and move on in your relationship to have the marriage you both desire.

How to Pray for Your Marriage

TWO ARE BETTER THAN ONE,...THOUGH ONE MAY BE
OVERPOWERED, TWO CAN DEFEND THEMSELVES.

Ecclesiastes 4:9,12

Praying for your partner and your marriage is of vital importance. Perhaps the most helpful way is to pray for God's will for your marriage. The best way to do this is to take God's Word and actually pray it for you and your partner. The following passages will show you how it can be done. The rest is up to you as you search the Scriptures each day.

I pray that my spouse and I will be swift to hear, slow to speak, slow to wrath; for the wrath of man does not produce the righteousness of God (James 1:19-20).

I pray that my spouse and I will always love the LORD our God with all our heart, with all our soul, with all our mind, and with all our strength and that we love our neighbor as ourselves (Mark 12:30-31).

I pray that when my spouse and I pass through the waters, You will be with us. And when we pass through the rivers, they shall not overflow us. When we walk through the fire, we shall not be burned, nor shall the flame scorch us (Isaiah 43:2).

I pray that my spouse and I will always remember that faith is the substance of things hoped for, the evidence of things not seen (Hebrews 11:1).

I pray that my spouse and I will bring all the tithes into the storehouse, that there may be food in Your house. And that we will try You, God, in this and see if You will not open for us the windows of heaven and pour out for us such blessing that there will not be room enough to receive it (Malachi 3:10).

I pray that this Book of the Law shall not depart

from my spouse's and my mouths, but that we shall meditate in it day and night, that we may observe to do according to all that is written in it. For then we will make our way prosperous, and then we will have good success (Joshua 1:8).

I pray that my spouse and I will present our bodies a living sacrifice, holy, acceptable to You, God (Romans 12:1).

I pray that my spouse and I will not be conformed to this world, but that we will be transformed by the renewing of our minds, that we may prove what is that good and acceptable and perfect will of God (Romans 12:2).

I pray that my spouse and I love Your commandments, Jesus, and keep them, as those who love You. And because we love You, we will be loved by Your Father, and You will love us and manifest Yourself to us (John 14:21).

I pray, Jesus, that my spouse and I will follow Your commandment, that we love one another as You have loved us (John 15:12).

I pray that my spouse and I will always understand the significance of the question, "Can two walk together, unless they are agreed?" (Amos 3:3).

I pray that the fruit of the Spirit in my spouse and me is love, joy, peace, longsuffering, kindness, goodness, faithfulness, gentleness, self-control (Galatians 5:22-23).

I pray that my spouse and I do not forget You, the LORD our God, by not keeping Your commandments, Your judgement, and Your statues which You command us today. I pray that we shall remember You, the LORD our God, for it is You who gives us the power to get wealth (Deuteronomy 8:11,17).[1]

Note
1. Lee Roberts, *Praying God's Will for My Marriage* (Nashville: Thomas Nelson Publishers, 1994), pp. 1, 9, 19, 28, 115, 162, 227, 267. Scripture references taken from the *New King James Version*.

Avoid the "Takens" in Your Marriage

"AND WHATEVER YOU DO [NO MATTER WHAT IT IS]
IN WORD OR DEED, DO EVERYTHING IN THE NAME
OF THE LORD JESUS AND IN [DEPENDENCE UPON]
HIS PERSON, GIVING PRAISE TO GOD THE
FATHER THROUGH HIM."

Colossians 3:17 (Amp.)

A major positive in your marriage will be to never become complacent or take one another for granted. A friend of mine described it this way:

> People in long-term marriages tend to take each other for granted. The most common of the "takens" include:
> You will always be here for me.
> You will always love me.
> You will always be able to provide for me.
> You will always be the same.
> We will always be together.
> Making these assumptions in a marriage is living more in fantasyland than on reality ridge. People who take things for granted are seldom appreciative of the everyday blessings in their lives. After a time, they come to believe life owes them these little gifts. They seldom say thank you for anything.
> When you take someone for granted you demean him or her. You send the unspoken message: You are not worth much to me. You also rob this person of the gift of human appreciation. And to be loved and appreciated gives all of us a reason to live each day. When that gift is withdrawn or denied over the years, our spirits wither and die. People may endure this hardship and stay married forever, but they are

only serving a sentence. In long-term marriages where one or both spouses are continually taken for granted, a wall of indifference arises between husband and wife. The longer the marriage, the higher the wall and the greater the human isolation. The way out of this woodpile is simple but crucial:

Start saying thank you and showing appreciation for anything and everything.

Be more consciously tuned in to what is going on around you.

Become more giving and affirming.

Specialize in the many little things that mean a lot: Bring each other flowers, take long walks in the country, lie on the floor in front of the fireplace, prepare breakfast in bed for each other, hold hands in public and walk in the rain, send caring and funny cards to each other in the mail, buy each other small gifts for no apparent reason.

Remember: A thirty-five year marriage does not guarantee year number thirty-six. Take nothing for granted just because you have it today.[1]

Keep in mind that in a healthy marriage...

You look out for "number 2" rather than number 1.

You energize your spouse rather than drain energy from him or her.

You eliminate blaming and shaming from the marriage.

You are willing to learn from your partner.

You end your disagreements with a feeling of resolve.

You feel better after a disagreement.[2]

These are just some of the positives that will keep your marriage alive.

Notes

1. Jim Smoke, *Facing 50* (Nashville: Thomas Nelson Publishers, 1994), pp. 40-41.
2. Paul Pearsall, *The Ten Laws of Lasting Love* (New York: Simon & Schuster, 1993), pp. 298-299, adapted.

THIRTY-EIGHT

Respect One Another

NEVERTHELESS LET EACH INDIVIDUAL AMONG YOU ALSO
LOVE HIS OWN WIFE EVEN AS HIMSELF; AND LET THE
WIFE SEE TO IT THAT SHE RESPECT HER HUSBAND.

Ephesians 5:33 (NASB)

Do you remember the comedian who used to say, "I just don't get no respect"? We laughed about it, but how many people really know what respect is? Dictionaries say "respect" means to feel or show honor or esteem for a person, to hold them in high regard, to treat with deference, to show consideration for. In marriage, respect means you notice things about your partner that no one else does. God's Word calls you to love one another as you love yourself and to respect each other.

Will you have a respectful marriage? This is part of our calling as believers. The Scripture passage for today instructs both husbands and wives to respond to one another with respect. Do you understand what that means in marriage? Respect in marriage means ministering to your partner through listening, a loving embrace, a flexible mind and attitude and a gracious spirit. It means looking past faults and differences and seeing strengths and similarities. It means sharing concerns mutually instead of attempting to carry the load yourself.

Consider the following questions as you evaluate your respect for one another now and in the future:

- In a tense situation, do I cut off my partner when he or she holds a view different from mine?
- When I think my partner is wrong, do I become offensive and harsh trying to put him or her in place?
- In trying to get a point across, am I gently persuasive or opinionated and demanding?
- Am I driven so much by the need to be right that I try to pressure my spouse into my position? Do I intimidate my partner?

- Do I ever interrupt my partner when he or she takes too long to respond?
- Do I ever put my partner down in public or make fun of him or her so that it hurts?
- Do I get irritated because my partner's thinking or communication style is different from my own?[1]

Yes, these are questions that meddle. But answering them is a good step toward building a respectful marriage. As one author said, respect begins when we "learn to practice careful listening rather than threatened opposition, honest expression rather than resentment, flexibility rather than rigidity, loving censure rather than harsh coercion, encouragement rather than intimidation."[2]

True respect creates space for your partner to develop individuality and potential. It creates rather then restricts freedom. How will the respect be in your marriage relationship?

Notes
1. Judith C. Lechman, "Love as Respect," in Howard and Jeanne Hendricks, eds., *Husbands and Wives* (Wheaton, Ill.: Victor Books, 1988), p. 47.
2. Ibid., pp. 46, 47, adapted.

An Unchanging God

I THE LORD DO NOT CHANGE. SO YOU, O DESCEN-
DANTS OF JACOB, ARE NOT DESTROYED.

Malachi 3:6

We live in a world full of rapid change; and it is occurring faster and faster. One thing though does not and will not change, and that is God. Change has a purpose; it is either for better or for worse. It is impossible, however, for God to change. What does that actually mean?

God's life does not change. Created things have a beginning and an ending, but God does not. He has always been. At no time did He not exist. He does not grow older. He does not get wiser, stronger or weaker. He cannot change for the better. He is already there.

> They shall perish, but you go on forever. They will grow old, like worn-out clothing, and you will change them like a man putting on a new shirt and throwing away the old one! (Ps. 102:26, *TLB*).
>
> Listen to me, my people, my chosen ones! I alone am God. I am the First; I am the Last (Isa. 48:12, *TLB*).

God's *character* does not change. He does not become less or more truthful, merciful or good than He was or is. James talks about God's goodness, holiness and generosity to men. He speaks about God as one "with whom there is no variation or shadow due to change" (Jas. 1:17, *RSV*).

God's *truth* does not change. He does not have to take back anything He has ever said. God still keeps the promises of His Word.

God's *purposes* do not change. What God does in the context of time, He planned from eternity. All He has committed Himself to do in His Word will be done.

One of God's characteristics is His immutability. We need

to pray in harmony with His character. Let's consider some of God's character traits and what they mean for our prayers:

God is holy, so we must never pray for anything that would compromise His holiness or cause us to be unholy (Psalm 99:9; Isaiah 6:3; Revelation 15:4).

God is love, and our prayers should both invoke the love of God for others and reflect the love of God in our own attitudes (Jeremiah 31:3; John 3:16; Romans 5:8).

God is good, and the results of our prayers must bring goodness into the lives of all concerned (Psalm 25:8; 33:5; 34:8; Nahum 1:7; Matthew 19:17; Romans 2:4).

God is merciful, and our prayers should reflect that we have received His mercy and are willing to be merciful ourselves (Psalm 108:4; Lamentations 3:22; Joel 2:13).

God is jealous, and we dare not ask for something that would take first place in our hearts over God (Exodus 20:5; Deuteronomy 4:24; 1 Corinthians 10:22).

God is just, and we cannot expect Him to grant a request that would be unjust or unfair to anyone (Psalm 103:6; Zephaniah 3:5; John 5:30; Romans 2:2).

God is long-suffering, and neither our prayers nor our waiting for answers should show impatience toward Him who is so patient with us (Isaiah 48:9; Romans 9:22; 1 Peter 3:20).

God is truth, and our prayers must never seek to change or disguise truth (Deuteronomy 32:4; Romans 3:4; Hebrew 6:18).[1]

Spend a few minutes discussing how these traits will affect your prayers together, especially after you are married.

Note
1. Bill Austin, *How to Get What You Pray For* (Wheaton, Ill.: Tyndale House Publishers, 1984), p. 63.

In the Image of God

THEN GOD SAID, "LET US MAKE MAN IN OUR IMAGE."

Genesis 1:26

One day, perhaps not too long from now, you will be involved in a wedding ceremony. You may be the one standing at the front of the church watching a special person walking toward you or you may be the person doing the walking down the aisle. You may feel cool, calm and collected or you may have thousands of butterflies colliding in mass collisions in your stomach. You may have spent hours working on looking your best. You want to portray a certain image on that day. You want those in attendance to remember you by how you looked.

Who is that person your partner is about to marry? Who are you really? Who is that person with whom you will spend the rest of your life? Do you understand who you are and who that other special person is?

These are basic questions we tend to take for granted. If you were asked to tell who you are apart from any reference to your work or occupation, would you be able to do so? It is a stressful exercise for many people!

Sometimes our identity is all wrapped up in what we produce. Others have their identity built upon their status or their appearance. But God has a different perspective. The psalmist said, "When I consider your heavens, the work of your fingers, the moon and the stars, which you have set in place, what is man that you are mindful of him,...You made him a little lower than the heavenly beings and crowned him with glory and honor. You made him ruler over the works of your hands; you put everything under his feet" (Ps. 8:3-6). God does not use the criteria you do. He simply declares you to be someone special.

Why are humans so worthy? The answer is found in Genesis 1:26,27. Read these verses aloud together. We have this glory and majesty because of the way God created us.

FORTY

God gave us life, meaning, purpose and His presence to carry us through this life. You did not earn it. You can't earn it or buy it; it is an undeserved gift.

How does all this concern your marriage? Look at your future partner right now. You won't be living with just a marital partner, but with a person God created. He gave your partner the breath of life. Your calling is to care deeply and practically for that person, and as you do so your respect and your feelings for him or her will become more positive. The changes you see coming from this positive response will have a positive effect on both of your personalities.

Understand your partner and yourself through God's eyes. Remember who you are. Remember who your partner is. You both bear God's image. If you have children, they bear God's image as well. Just realizing that fact can affect how we think about another person and thus help change our behavior. That positive result makes our efforts to understand each other worthwhile.[1]

Note
1. H. Norman Wright, *Quiet Times for Couples* (Eugene, Oreg.: Harvest House Publishers, 1990), p. 323, adapted.

How Do You View God?

THE POT HE WAS SHAPING FROM THE CLAY WAS MARRED
IN HIS HANDS; SO THE POTTER FORMED IT INTO ANOTH-
ER POT, SHAPING IT AS SEEMED BEST TO HIM.

Jeremiah 18:4

What is your perception of God? How would your future partner describe God? Have the two of you ever shared your belief of who God is and what He is like? Sometimes we create God in our own image or in the image of our parents. If your own father was distant, impersonal and uncaring, and wouldn't intervene for you, you may see God as having the same characteristics.

If your father was a pushy man who was inconsiderate of you, or violated and used you, you may see God in the same way. If your father resembled a drill sergeant, and demanded more and more from you but expressed no satisfaction, or burned with anger and had no tolerance for mistakes, you may have cast God in his image.

If your father was a weakling, and you couldn't depend on him to help you or defend you, your image of God may be that of a weakling. If your father was overly critical and constantly came down hard on you, or if he didn't believe in you or your capabilities and discouraged you from trying, you may perceive God in the same way.

Consider the positive qualities of a father. Reflect on how these qualities, if they existed in your father, have positively influenced your perception of God. If your father was patient, you are more likely to see God as patient and available for you. You believe you are worth God's time and concern. If your father was kind, you probably see God acting kindly and graciously on your behalf. You believe you are worth God's help and intervention.

If your father was a giving man, you may perceive God as someone who gives to you and supports you. You believe you are worth God's support and encouragement. You believe God will give you what is best for you, and you respond by giving of yourself to others.

If your father accepted you, you tend to see God accepting you regardless of what you do. God does not dump on you or reject you when you struggle, but understands and encourages you. If your father protected you, you probably perceive God as your protector in life. You believe you are worthy of being under His care and you rest in His security.

Although we tend to do so, we cannot base our perceptions of God and our feelings about ourselves on how we were treated by our parents. Fathers and mothers are human and fallible—and some of them are prodigals! Our beliefs based on childhood experiences need to be cleansed out of our minds and emotions and replaced with the scriptural teaching about God.[1]

You will need an accurate perception of God for your sake and for the sake of your marriage.

Note
1. H. Norman Wright, *Always Daddy's Girl* (Ventura, Calif.: Regal Books, 1989), pp. 194-196, adapted.

What Is Forgiveness?

BEAR WITH EACH OTHER AND FORGIVE WHATEVER
GRIEVANCES YOU MAY HAVE AGAINST ONE ANOTHER.
FORGIVE AS THE LORD FORGAVE YOU.

Colossians 3:13

Many marriages are gradually eroded and eventually destroyed because one person is unable to forgive. A person who continually brings up something hurtful his spouse did or said in the past that was hurtful...continues to punish the other person and erects a wall of indifference and coldness.

If we know Jesus Christ as Savior, we have experienced God's forgiveness. Because we are in Christ, we have the capacity to forgive ourselves and thus are enabled to forgive others.

Forgiveness is not forgetting. God constructed you in such a way that your brain resembles a giant computer. Whatever has happened to you is stored in your memory. The remembrance will always be with you. There are, however, two different ways of remembering. One is to recall the offense or hurt in such a way that it continues to affect you and your relationship with another. It continues to eat away and bother you so that the hurt remains. Another way of remembering, however, simply says, "Yes, that happened. I know it did, but it no longer affects me. It's a fact of history, yet it has no emotional significance or effect. It is there, but we are progressing onward at this time and I am not hindered nor is our relationship hurt by that event." This is, in a sense, forgetting. The fact remains, but it no longer entangles you in its tentacles of control.

Forgiveness is not pretending. You cannot ignore the fact that an event occurred. Wishing it never happened will not make it go away. What has been done is done. Becoming a martyr and pretending ignorance of the event does not help the relationship. In fact, your lack of confrontation and reconciliation may encourage the other person to continue or repeat the same act or behavior.

Forgiveness is not a feeling. It is a clear and logical action on your part. It is not a soothing, comforting, overwhelming emotional response that erases the fact from your memory forever.

Forgiveness takes place when love accepts— deliberately—the hurts and abrasions of life and drops all charges against the other person. Forgiveness is accepting the other when both of you know he or she has done something unacceptable.

Forgiveness is smiling silent love to your partner when the justifications for keeping an insult or injury alive are on the tip of your tongue, yet you swallow them. Not because you have to, to keep peace, but because you want to, to make peace.

Forgiveness is not acceptance given "on condition" that the other become acceptable. Forgiveness is given freely. Out of the keen awareness that the forgiver also has a need of constant forgiveness, daily.

Forgiveness exercises God's strength to love and receives the other person without any assurance of complete restitution and making of amends.

Forgiveness is a relationship between equals who recognize their need of each other, share and share alike. Each needs the other's forgiveness. Each needs the other's acceptance. Each needs the other. And so, before God, each drops all charges, refuses all self-justification, and forgives. And forgives. Seventy times seven. As Jesus said.[1]

Note
1. David Augsburger, *Cherishable: Love and Marriage* (Scottdale, Pa.: Herald Press, 1976), p. 146.

Perfect Bodies? Someday

AND JUST AS WE HAVE BORNE THE LIKENESS
OF THE EARTHLY MAN, SO SHALL WE BEAR THE
LIKENESS OF THE MAN FROM HEAVEN.

1 Corinthians 15:49

Remember the first time you saw your future spouse? Bring that image back to mind. Where were you? What was the other wearing? What was your first impression and response to the way the person looked? It varies, you know. Some take that first look and say, "Wow! Yes! That's for me. I like it!" They are drawn to the physical appearance. Others are a bit more calm about it; whereas some have little response to the physical (or so they say).

People, however, are visual. It is important that you like what you see. Keep in mind that what you see now may change a bit over the years. There may be added pounds, glasses, hearing aids, blemishes, weight reduction and hair reduction. You will learn to make use of whatever is available to maintain your original appearance.

Look at your partner. Note his or her physical characteristics. What do you see? Right now you are still enjoying the excitement of physical attraction. Makeup, hair pieces and padded clothes all help to hide our physical frailties.

You will never be a perfect physical specimen in this life, nor will your partner. You may as well accept this fact. You can spend hours at the gym and that may be a good thing, but some bumps and blemishes will always be with you—the same for your partner. For that reason you will need to exercise a great deal of acceptance in your marriage. None of us is the Greek god or goddess our partner perceives us to be now. But that is all right. We are all in the same boat. Our worth and value to each other is not based upon our appearance—or it shouldn't be. If it is, we are in danger. Not only are we at the mercy of others, but we will also drive ourselves up a wall trying to perfect what was never perfect in the first place.

When it comes to our bodies, we can all relax. A day will come when they *will* be perfect. In eternity we will all have new bodies. We will be changed; and we won't be so concerned about how we look either. You are already a new person in Christ inwardly. The process of restoration has already begun on the inside. When you meet Jesus Christ face-to-face you will be complete.

Look at your body. Look at your partner's body. Tell each other, "It's all right to be incomplete physically now. Just wait. We were created in God's image and our physical bodies will be transformed when we die."

God's plan is for each of us to have a glorified body. It is just that His timing is a bit different from ours![1]

Note

1. H. Norman Wright, *Quiet Times for Couples* (Eugene, Oreg.: Harvest House Publishers, 1990), p. 275, adapted.

It's Time

BE MERCIFUL IN ACTION, KINDLY IN HEART,

HUMBLE IN MIND.

Colossians 3:12 (Phillips)

Time is a precious commodity for all of us. Too often, however, we take the time spent with our partners for granted.

"It's about time." "Have a good time." What time is it?" Where did time go?" These and other phrases are used again and again in our everyday conversations. We are all time oriented. The measurement of time has evolved into a status symbol as evidenced by Rolex watches. Your life is regulated by the clock. The theme of a famous song about weddings reflects this—"Get me to the church on time."

We all approach time differently. Some seem to have a built-in apparatus so they can tell you the time of day within five minutes without ever looking at a clock. Some are super punctual, whereas others don't know the meaning of the word. Some believe an event really hasn't started until they arrive, no matter how late they are. Some were created with a fast gear and others with a slow one. Some people go through life as though they were directed by a stopwatch, whereas others operate as though guided by a sundial. Think about time for a moment, as reflected in the following ideas.

Will you use time in a way that will bless your marriage? For example, will you thank God for His daily gift of time to you as man and wife? Time is, after all, the invaluable raw material of your marriage. You wake up in the morning and it is always there—24 precious hours to spend as you choose. Will you live and love one another as if it were the last day to enjoy your gift of time? What would you do if you knew you were spending your final 24 hours together? What would you say? How would you act toward one another?

Will you regularly invite God into your precious slice of time together? Have you started to gain His vision of what He wants to do with your future relationship?

FORTY-FOUR

Will you practice mutuality each day? That is, will you adapt, accept, forgive, always making all things mutual in the spirit of loving give and take? That is what it is all about.

Will you value the ordinary days—including the dull routine—of living together? Will you trade 1 ordinary day with your partner for 10 "exciting" ones without him or her? Be careful how you answer. Some couples do just that and call it "working extra hard at the office" or "pouring myself into the children."

Will you make sure you don't allow the greatest sin of all—wasting your time together on self-centeredness, self-justification, self-advancement, self-pity, self-aggrandizement and self-righteousness—to involve your marriage? Your time is far too precious for that.[1]

Note
1. Fritz Ridenour, ed., *The Marriage Collection* (Grand Rapids: Zondervan Publishers, 1989), pp. 396, 397, adapted.

You Have Been Chosen

PRAISE BE TO THE GOD AND FATHER OF OUR LORD
JESUS CHRIST, WHO HAS BLESSED US IN THE HEAVENLY
REALMS WITH EVERY SPIRITUAL BLESSING IN CHRIST.
FOR HE CHOSE US IN HIM BEFORE THE CREATION OF
THE WORLD TO BE HOLY AND BLAMELESS IN HIS SIGHT.

Ephesians 1:3,4

One of the delights of marrying is to realize that someone chose you. You are so desired and special that someone wants to spend the rest of his or her life with *you*! Someone else chose you a long time ago—God. You were chosen by God. His selection of you has nothing to do with any of your characteristics or qualities. God chose to declare you holy and blameless before Him apart from your merits and despite your shortcomings. God simply chose you to be with Him. Why did He do this? Because He loves you.

Remember back when you were a bit younger (perhaps a *lot* younger), when you were in grade school and had to play on teams? Next to being the captain of the team, what was the best thing that could happen? Wasn't it being the first one chosen? Of course, it is possible you were never the first one chosen. Maybe you were always the last. The good news is that those days have ended. You are the object of God's attention.

Our understanding of who God is and how He wants to bless our lives is enriched when we realize He is committed to performing good in our lives. In his fascinating book *The Pleasures of God*, John Piper beautifully expresses how God desires to do good to all who hope in Him. Dr. Piper talks about God singing and asks, "What would it be like if God sang?" What do you hear when you imagine the voice of God singing?

"I hear the booming of Niagara Falls mingled with the trickle of a mossy mountain stream. I hear the blast of Mt. Saint Helens mingled with a kitten's purr. I hear the power of an East Coast hurricane and the barely audible puff of a night snow in the woods. And I hear the unimaginable roar of the sun, 865,000 miles thick, 1,300,000 times bigger than the earth, and nothing but fire, 1,000,000 degrees centigrade on the cooler surface of the corona. But I hear this unimaginable roar mingled with the tender, warm crackling of logs in the living room on a cozy winter's night.

"I stand dumbfounded, staggered, speechless that he is singing over me—one who has dishonored him so many times and in so many ways. It is almost too good to be true. He is rejoicing over my good with all his heart and all his soul. He virtually breaks forth into song when he hits upon a new way to do me good."[1]

Did you catch the significance of how God feels about you and what He wants for you? Do you get a sense of the blessing for which you have been created and chosen?

Dr. Piper compares our relationship with God to a marriage. He goes on to talk about how the honeymoon ends for all married couples. Reality sets in and the level of honeymoon intensity and affection diminishes. The two people change, and defects become more apparent. But it is different with God:

"God says his joy of his people is like a bridegroom over a bride. He is talking about honeymoon intensity and honeymoon pleasures and honeymoon energy and excitement and enthusiasm and enjoyment. He is trying to get into our hearts what he means when he says he rejoices over us *with all his heart*. And to add to this, with God the honeymoon never ends. He is infinite in power and wisdom and creativity and love. And so he has no trouble sustaining a honeymoon level of intensity; he can foresee all the future quirks of our personality and has decided he will keep what's good for us and change what isn't."[2]

Does that say something to you about your value and worth?[3]

Notes
1. John Piper, *The Pleasures of God* (Portland, Oreg.: Multnomah Press, 1991), p. 188.
2. Ibid., p. 195.
3. H. Norman Wright, *Chosen for Blessing* (Eugene, Oreg.: Harvest House Publishers, 1992), pp. 12-15, adapted.

You Are Marrying an Adopted Child

YET TO ALL WHO RECEIVED HIM, TO THOSE WHO
BELIEVED IN HIS NAME, HE GAVE THE RIGHT TO
BECOME CHILDREN OF GOD.

John 1:12

You are marrying an adopted child. Surprised? Well, it is true. When you or your partner invited Jesus Christ into your lives you were adopted into God's family. That is what John was writing about in today's verse. Being adopted is a good thing. It means you are no stranger to God. You are a distant relative. He has chosen *you* to be His child.

Romans 8:16 states: "The Spirit himself testifies with our spirit that we are God's children." When you understand the fullness of your spiritual adoption, it can redirect your thinking and response to life. Your adoption is a gift of grace.

Did you know that in Roman law during New Testament times it was common practice for a childless adult who wanted an heir to adopt an adult male as his son? You too have been adopted by God as His heir. The apostle Paul wrote: "Now if we are children, then we are heirs—heirs of God and co-heirs with Christ" (Rom. 8:17). "So you are no longer a slave, but a son; and since you are a son, God has made you also an heir" (Gal. 4:7).

Perhaps you remember the book or the movie *Ben Hur*? Judah Ben Hur was a Jewish slave until the Roman admiral, Arias, adopted him. Judah was given all the rights and privileges of full sonship. He was accepted by Arias as if he had been born into the family. Similarly, when you received Jesus Christ as your Savior, you were adopted into God's family and received all the rights and privileges of a full heir.

What are some of the rights and privilege you inherited? The book of Ephesians lists some of these rights:

- You have been guaranteed eternal life, as evidenced by the presence of the Holy Spirit in your life (see 1:14).
- You have hope in Christ, your glorious inheritance (see 1:18).
- You have experienced the incomparable power that raised Jesus Christ from the dead and seated Him at God's right hand (see 1:19,20).
- You are the recipient of God's incomparable grace that saved you apart from anything you have done or can ever do (see 2:8,9).
- You now have access to the Father through His Spirit (see 2:18).
- You can know the love of Christ that will enable you to receive God's fullness (see 3:19).

How do you feel about being adopted by the King of the universe and being delivered from the kingdom of darkness (see Col. 1:13)? This is one of the greatest blessings the gospel offers to you. You have been taken into God's family and fellowship, and you have been established as His child and heir. You may have come from a dysfunctional home. Perhaps you experienced emotional or physical abuse in your natural family. But God is a Father who can fill the gaps in your life because of who He is and what He has done for you. Because you are in a family, closeness, affection and generosity are the basis of your relationship with Father God. You are loved and cared for by your Father. Your relationship as an heir is the basis for your Christian life. It can help you respond in a healthy, loving way to your prospective partner for the next 50 years![1]

Note
1. H. Norman Wright, *Chosen for Blessing* (Eugene, Oreg.: Harvest House Publishers, 1992), pp. 36-38, adapted.

Marriage Is Not for Victims

I CAN DO EVERYTHING THROUGH HIM WHO GIVES ME STRENGTH.

Philippians 4:13

We hear a lot today about victims; and they do exist because of what others have done to them. Some people, however, are self-made victims because of what they have chosen to believe. These beliefs cripple their own growth and development as well as hamper the health of their marriage. It may be well to identify these thoughts and phrases so they never have an opportunity to creep into your life. When they exist, every time they are used you subconsciously began to believe and fulfill them.

"I can't." Have you ever kept track of how often you say this? Do you realize that these words are prompted by some kind of unbelief, fear or lack of hope? Think about it. These three factors often hinder us from moving on with our lives and marriage. When you say, "I can't," you are saying you have no control of your life. But it's no harder to say, "It's worth a try." You will like the results of this positive phrase much better.

"That's a problem." Sometimes instead of saying, "That's a problem," we say, "He's a problem" or "She's a problem," especially after being married for a while. People who see life's complications as problems or burdens are immersed in fear and hopelessness. Life is full of barriers and detours, but every obstacle presents an opportunity to learn and grow—if you have the right attitude. Using other phrases such as "That's a challenge" or "That's an opportunity for learning something new" leaves the door open for moving ahead.

"I'll never..." This victim phrase is the anchor of personal stagnation. It is the signal of unconditional surrender to what exists or has happened in your life. It does not give yourself or God an opportunity. Instead say, "I've never considered that before" or "I haven't tried it, but I'm willing to try" and open the door to personal growth.

FORTY-SEVEN

"Why is life this way?" This is a normal response to the deep pains and sudden shocks of life. Some people experience one hurt and disappointment after another. Others experience a major setback and choose to linger in its crippling aftermath without recovering. They inappropriately use this question again and again for months and years.

"Why is life this way?" and its companion statement, "Life isn't fair," are overused for the normal, minor upsets of everyday life. Life *is* unpredictable. Life *is* unfair. Life *is not* always the way we want it to be. But our response to life is our choice, and the healthiest response is reflected in James 1:2,3. These verses encourage us to consider adversity as something to welcome or be glad about. Joy in life is a choice. Growth in life is a choice. Change in life can be a choice, and choice comes before joy, growth and change.

"If only..." This phrase imprisons us in lost dreams. Another phrase, however, can release us from yesterday and usher us into the future. The phrase "next time" shows that we have given up our regrets, we have learned from past experiences and we are continuing on with our lives.

"Life is a big struggle." This victim phrase reinforces the difficulties of life. Struggles can and should be turned into adventures. Your future marriage could be structured either way. Yes, it will take work. You may be stretched, and you may feel uncomfortable for a time. But this is the way to take steps forward.

"What will I do?" This question is a cry of despair coupled with fear of the future and the unknown. Instead say, "I don't know what I can do at this moment, but I know I can handle this. Thank God I don't have to face this issue by myself. I can learn and become a different person." Remember the encouraging words in Jeremiah 29:11: "'For I know the plans I have for you,' declares the Lord, 'plans to prosper you and not to harm you, plans to give you hope and a future.'"[1]

Note

1. H. Norman Wright, *Chosen for Blessing* (Eugene, Oreg.: Harvest House Publishers, 1992), pp. 118-120, adapted.

Your Memories and Your Marriage

I AM AGAIN IN THE PAINS OF CHILDBIRTH UNTIL
CHRIST IS FORMED IN YOU.

Galatians 4:19

Memories. Life is made of them—some good and some bad. A marriage is made of memories. Some of your memories you create together deliberately; others just seem to happen. Some will be funny; others will be sad. Some you wish you had more of; whereas others you could do without.

Sometimes the memories you bring with you into the marriage tend to haunt your marriage. They may be hurts you or your partner experienced early in life. When you come to marriage, some of these wounds are not healed; they are merely covered by scabs. These unhealed emotional wounds tend to erupt when other difficulties in marriage rip off the scabs. Remember—whatever unresolved issues you bring into your marriage won't go away. They will be dormant but alive, just waiting for some situation to give them life again. Often memories from the past interfere with your enjoyment of the present.

The way you remember what happened in the past is important. Often our memories become distorted as time passes. In one of his sermons, Dr. Lloyd Ogilvie, chaplain of the United States Senate, said, "We mortgage the future based upon what happened in the past. We have positive memories of the past which we can't imagine could ever be repeated, and we have negative memories which we know will be repeated. Often we become the image of what we remember instead of what we envision for the future!"

What about you and your future partner? Do either of you have memories that interfere with your life or could hamper your marriage? Is the future of your marriage mortgaged on memories from the past? Have you not shared some experiences with your future partner? Something the person will discover?

To overcome a past hurt, you have to lower the walls you have built around the hurt and confront those concerns. Sometimes the change is immediate, but more often than not healing is a slow process. You can take down the walls of protection because of the presence of Christ in your life. Change is possible because our faith involves inner transformation, not just outer conformity. That is what the verse for today exemplifies. Your new life in Christ is put on from the inside.

Reflect on the ways God's presence in your life has already changed your life. For continual growth, give Him access to your painful memories. A slow process? Yes, but it is worth every bit of the time and energy you will invest. Healing your memories will not only benefit you, but your marriage as well.

Let God's Word Rule Your Marriage

LET THE PEACE OF CHRIST RULE IN YOUR HEARTS, SINCE
AS MEMBERS OF ONE BODY YOU WERE CALLED TO PEACE.
AND BE THANKFUL. LET THE WORD OF CHRIST DWELL IN
YOU RICHLY AS YOU TEACH AND ADMONISH ONE ANOTHER
WITH ALL WISDOM, AND AS YOU SING PSALMS, HYMNS
AND SPIRITUAL SONGS WITH GRATITUDE IN YOUR HEARTS
TO GOD. AND WHATEVER YOU DO, WHETHER IN WORD OR
DEED, DO IT ALL IN THE NAME OF THE LORD JESUS, GIV-
ING THANKS TO GOD THE FATHER THROUGH HIM.

Colossians 3:15-17

No one marries wanting to have a marriage filled with has-
sles, quarrels, fights, upsets and tension. Every person wants
a harmonious, loving and peaceful relationship; and it is
possible. Paul talked about it in the opening verses from
Colossians. These verses will do wonders for your marriage
if you understand and apply them. Think about them.

Let the peace of Christ rule. The peace described here is not
just the peace you experience when you have no conflict. It
is a sense of wholeness and well-being. When Christ rules,
you feel complete. This phrase could be paraphrased, "Let
the peace of Christ be umpire in your heart amidst the conflicts of life. Let Christ's peace within decide what is right.
Let it be your counselor."

Who or what rules in your life? Perhaps if we allow the
peace of Christ to rule in our hearts, the hurtful words we
feel like saying in the midst of a conflict would never be said.
The indwelling peace of Christ is indispensable to responding to your partner in a loving way.

Let the Word of Christ dwell in you. How does God's Word
abide in us? By reading it, studying it and memorizing it.

Angry people have changed because of God's Word.

Frustrated people have changed because of God's Word.
Anxious people have changed because of God's Word.
Obnoxious people have changed because of God's Word.
God's Word changes us. When you read it, ask the Holy
spirit to make it a part of your life.

The truths of Scripture can counter the false beliefs we
have about ourselves, God and other beliefs we were taught
or have learned in some way.[1]

Dr. Kenneth Boa writes:

> The affirmations of Scripture encourage us to walk by
> faith, not by feelings, and tell us the way things really
> are regardless of our emotional, cultural, and theolog-
> ical filters. Our circumstances may threaten our com-
> mitment to the truths that God is in control of our
> affairs and has our best interest at heart, but Scripture
> affirms these foundational principles and tells us to
> cling to them even in the midst of life's pain.
>
> These affirmations are not a matter of wishful
> thinking; they are true of every person who places his
> or her hope in Jesus Christ. They stress our identity in
> Christ, tell us that process is more important than
> product, and challenge us to value relationships more
> than objectives. They teach us that what we do does
> not determine who we are; rather, our being should
> shape our doing. They reinforce the realistic perspec-
> tive that we are aliens and pilgrims, not citizens of this
> world, and tell us to walk in grace and live in the
> power of the Spirit of God instead of walking in obe-
> dience to a set of external rules and living in the power
> of the flesh. They counsel us to take the risks of apply-
> ing biblical precepts and principles and to place our
> hope in the character and promises of God, and not in
> the people, possessions, or prestige of this world.[2]

Consider and adapt these ideas into your relationship.

Notes
1. Kenneth Boa, *Night Light* (Brentwood, Tenn.: Wolgemuth and Hyatt
   Publishers, Inc., 1989), p. 2, adapted.
2. Ibid., p. 2.

Renew Your Marriage

WE ARE BEING RENEWED DAY BY DAY.

2 Corinthians 4:16

BE MADE NEW IN THE ATTITUDE OF YOUR MINDS.

Ephesians 4:23

Renewal is a part of our lives. Whether we realize it or not, we are constantly in the process of renewing some element of our lives.

Do you know what renewal means? The dictionary says to renew is to make something like new, to give it new vigor or to make it fresh. Something comes alive during renewal. Renewal signifies growth. The opposite is stagnation and decay.

Houses in a state of decay come alive through the process of renewal; so do businesses and ministries. Renewal, though, sparks greater excitement in two other areas: our individual lives and our marriages.

Individual lives in a state of stagnation and decay come alive when we confront Jesus Christ. His presence produces renewal and makes our lives fresh. In his letter to the Ephesians, Paul states that we are able to put aside the old way of life and put on the new way of life (4:22-24):

> You were taught, with regard to your former way of life, to put off your old self, which is being corrupted by its deceitful desires; to be made new in the attitude of your minds; and to put on the new self, created to be like God in true righteousness and holiness.

This process creates a renewal of our minds.

Each year you receive renewal notices from magazines, newspapers, organizations and the list goes on.

Marriages, too, can come alive. I have seen stagnating, decaying marriages begin to blossom and come alive as they were renewed in Christ. They became fresh and alive. A new sense of love, romance, intimacy, commitment, trust and hope appears.

What about your marriage? Will renewal occur? Where will you need it to occur? How will your partner like your marriage to be renewed? Hard questions? Perhaps. Premarital questions? No. They are necessary questions. Begin by asking God for guidance, and then talk about these hard questions as a couple.

Romans 12:2 states:

> Do not conform any longer to the pattern of this world, but be transformed by the renewing of your mind. Then you will be able to test and approve what God's will is—his good, pleasing and perfect will.

At times in your married years you will need renewal. Do not let problems and issues build up until you need massive reconstruction. Be involved in a process of renewal. Remember—marriage needs acts of daily creation. Make your marriage come alive, not yearly, not monthly, not weekly, but daily.

What Will You Give Up When You Marry?

JESUS LOOKED AT HIM AND LOVED HIM. "ONE THING
YOU LACK," HE SAID. "GO, SELL EVERYTHING YOU
HAVE AND GIVE TO THE POOR, AND YOU WILL HAVE
TREASURE IN HEAVEN. THEN COME, FOLLOW ME."

Mark 10:21

What did you give up to marry your partner? Have you ever thought about it? Some people think they are giving up their freedom! Many people today simply try to bring their single lifestyles into their marriage relationships. They think a marriage partner is just one more addition to their already busy lives. They believe they will somehow be able to fit in a husband or wife around everything else. For example, they may continue to go to the gym four nights a week to work out by themselves, or go out with friends three times a week without the partner.

A rude awakening occurs when the truth of what marriage really is penetrates these people: "A marriage is not a joining of two worlds, but an abandoning of two worlds in order that one new one might be formed. In this sense, the call to be married bears comparison to Jesus' advice to the rich young man to sell all his possessions and to follow Him. It is a vocation to total abandonment."[1]

When you marry, you will have to make some adjustments and change a few habits. Perhaps you may put some educational dreams on hold for a while or delay buying something you have wanted for a long time. As Jesus' message to the rich young ruler illustrates, true commitment to someone means much more than that. When you marry, you will begin to fulfill one of Jesus' commands. Mike Mason relates: "For most people...marriage is the single most wholehearted step they will ever take toward a fulfillment of Jesus' command to love one's neighbor, and often enough a neighbor who has been left beaten and wounded on the road of love, whom all the rest of the world has in a sense passed by."[2]

How can you be faithful in fulfilling the commands of Jesus to love your partner selflessly? It means:

- Doing what your partner prefers for an evening;
- Watching a TV program your partner prefers to watch;
- Cooking a meal the way your partner likes it rather than the way you have always had it;
- Going shopping the way your partner enjoys to shop;
- Listening to your partner more than you think is necessary;
- Protecting your partner from an embarrassing situation;
- Attending an activity you never dreamed you would ever attend, because it is a favorite of your partner;
- Not going to the favorite vacation spot you have been going to for the past 17 years, but being willing to try something totally new;
- Learning to love the animals your partner loves and dividing the house and yard into an animals-allowed section and a no-trespassing area;
- Learning to either expand or diminish your level of input depending upon the communication style of your partner;
- Hanging up your clothes and rinsing your dishes immediately, although this was not done in your home as you were being raised.

Whatever it is, large or small, it can't be imagined or fulfilled without the grace and love of God. What a tragedy if His grace were not available. Thank God for His continuing grace.

Notes
1. Mike Mason, *The Mystery of Marriage* (Portland, Oreg.: Multnomah Press, 1985), p. 91.
2. Ibid.

See as God Sees

"DO YOU HAVE EYES BUT FAIL TO SEE?"

Mark 8:18

Eyes—we use them to scan the room, to focus so intently on someone that everything else begins to blur. Our eyes tell us stories. They invite people into our lives. Your eyes were an important instrument in bringing you to marriage. In his book *The Mystery of Marriage*, Mike Mason says:

> Marriage is, before it is anything else, an act of contemplation. It is a divine pondering, an exercise in amazement. This is evident from the very start, from the moment a man and a woman first lay eyes on one another and realize they are in love. The whole thing begins with a wondrous looking, a helpless staring, an irresistible compulsion simply to behold. For suddenly there is so much to see! So much is revealed when two people dare to stand in the radiance of one another's love. And so there is a divine paralysis of adoration; everything else stops, or at least fades into the background, and love itself takes center stage.[1]

Marital vows today seem to have less meaning and commitment to the marrying couple than they did a generation ago. A vow is supposed to be binding regardless of personal need fulfillment, lack of love, the attraction of another or incapacitating illness. Couples need to commit to a fidelity without any qualifications, limitations or restrictions. For some, making a serious marital vow is difficult, for they have little experience in being faithful to anything or anyone and are not aware of the high cost. Without the promise of fidelity, there can be no trust.[2]

When couples marry they are called to be faithful; but to what? We are called to faithfulness in all areas of our lives:

to marriage itself as a calling; to the friendship phase of the marital relationship so that each comes to see the other as his or her best friend; to our partner as a child of God, a joint heir with us. We are admonished to treat each other as such. Part of our calling in life is to minister to others in the name of Jesus Christ, and this means our partners as well.

Remember the phrase in the old wedding ceremony, which says: "I plight thee my troth"? The word "troth" is an old English term that carries with it the pledge to be true, faithful, loyal and honest. It also involves trust, reliability and integrity. Troth carries with it the possibility of mutual intimacy, deep communication, the ability to trust and depend upon each other. To "plight thee my troth" means that I will actively work to include all these characteristics in my marital relationship.[3]

Notes

1. Mike Mason, *The Mystery of Marriage* (Portland, Oreg.: Multnomah Press, 1985), p. 29.
2. H. Norman Wright, *Seasons of a Marriage* (Ventura, Calif.: Regal Books, 1982), pp. 104-105, adapted.
3. Ibid., pp. 102-103, adapted.

Leave and Cleave

FOR THIS CAUSE A MAN SHALL LEAVE HIS FATHER AND
HIS MOTHER, AND SHALL CLEAVE TO HIS WIFE; AND
THEY SHALL BECOME ONE FLESH.

Genesis 2:24 (NASB)

"Leave" and "cleave"—different words, significant words. When you exchange your wedding vows, these two words will become part of your life. But do you understand them? To leave means to sever one relationship before establishing another. In the Hebrew, it means literally to abandon or forsake. This does not mean you disregard your parents. Rather, it requires that you break your tie to them and assume responsibility for your spouse.

How much do your parents influence your life now? How much will they influence you in the future? How often do you plan to call or visit them? Will parents or you and your partner decide where to spend Thanksgiving and Christmas? Will you ever borrow money from them or live with them? Will you ever complain to them about your partner? Do you plan to visit them each year for your vacation? These are just a few simple but necessary questions you need to ask and answer! Leave means just that—but it is more than just physical leaving; it is emotional as well.

Consider the other word in this passage.

To cleave means to weld together. When a man cleaves to his wife they become one flesh. This term is a beautiful capsule description of the oneness, completeness and permanence God intended in the marriage relationship. It suggests a unique oneness—a total commitment to intimacy in all of life together, symbolized by the sexual union.

Years ago I heard a choice description of the coming together involved in cleaving. If you hold a lump of dark green clay in one hand and a lump of light green clay in the other hand, you can clearly identify the two different shades of color. When you mold the two lumps together, however, you see just one lump of green clay—at first glance. When you inspect the lump closely, you see the distinct and separate lines of dark and light green clay.

This is a picture of you in your marriage relationship. The two of you will be blended together so you will appear as one, yet you will each retain your own distinct identity and personality. You will have a marriage personality that exists in the two of you.

A Christian marriage, however, involves more than blending two people. It also includes a third person—Jesus Christ—who gives meaning, guidance and direction to the relationship. When He presides in a marriage, then and only then is it a Christian marriage. Jesus needs to be closer to you than you will be to each other.

After your wedding, how will you handle leaving your parents? How will you become one flesh, coming together and yet retaining who you are as individuals? Why not talk about it?[1]

Note

1. H. Norman Wright, *Quiet Times for Couples* (Eugene, Oreg.: Harvest House Publishers, 1990), p. 9, adapted.

Money and Your Marriage— Curse or Blessing?

FOR THE LOVE OF MONEY IS A ROOT OF ALL KINDS
OF EVIL. SOME PEOPLE, EAGER FOR MONEY,
HAVE WANDERED FROM THE FAITH AND PIERCED
THEMSELVES WITH MANY GRIEFS.

1 Timothy 6:10

The number-one conflict during the first year of marriage is money. Some of your biggest disagreements may be about money, but they do not have to be. Why does this happen? We all have different spending and saving styles. This is a reflection of our personalities.

Did you realize that money can be a weapon of independence? It can be the reason for arguments about responsibility and judgment. It can be used as a source of power and control. Money not only buys clothes, cars, computers and stocks, but it can also buy power. Money can be a reflection of one's self-worth. Spending can be a way to help yourself feel good, to get your partner's attention or to get back at him or her!

We all need money. Prices climb and the paycheck shrinks. The battle gets especially rough as you take on the payments of a home, car and then kids. How will you save for a college education when tuition at many schools can cost as much as $12,000 to $16,000 a year? How will you pay off your own school loans or credit cards? How do you continue to pay the bills when the expenses are too high? It is a struggle for all of us.

Some people have a different kind of problem with money—they love it. It becomes the reason for their existence, the source of their ambitions, their goal in life. Money is their god.

What part does money play in your life? Think about the following questions:

- What percentage of the day do you spend worrying about money?
- Do you spend more time thinking or worrying about money than you spend praying each day?
- When you are feeling down, discouraged or hurt, do you jump in the car and go on a shopping spree to help make you feel better?
- Do you wish your partner were more frugal, or would spend more?
- Do you have a specific plan for how much money you can spend each month when you are married?
- Who will be responsible for handling the money after you are married?
- Does the value you attach to yourself as a person fluctuate in accordance with the fluctuation of your net worth?
- To what extent has money been the source of arguments between you and other family members in your family of origin?
- If you listed all your canceled checks, what message would they tell about the place money has in your life?
- In the home you are leaving, to what extent have you operated on a well-defined budget that the entire family is aware of and has some voice in creating?
- To what extent do you have a plan to handle extra money that comes in unexpectedly? (That does happen, you know.)
- To what extent will you and your partner pray about money and the direction God wants you to take in using it for His kingdom and glory?

Think about these questions and develop some answers with your future partner.

When Tough Times Come

THIS IS WHAT THE LORD SAYS: "LET NOT THE WISE MAN
BOAST OF HIS WISDOM OR THE STRONG MAN BOAST OF HIS
STRENGTH OR THE RICH MAN BOAST OF HIS RICHES, BUT
LET HIM WHO BOASTS BOAST ABOUT THIS: THAT HE
UNDERSTANDS AND KNOWS ME, THAT I AM THE LORD, WHO
EXERCISES KINDNESS, JUSTICE AND RIGHTEOUSNESS ON
EARTH, FOR IN THESE I DELIGHT," DECLARES THE LORD.

Jeremiah 9:23,24

Some rough and tough times may invade your marriage. Life is not smooth; upsets will come. You may wonder what the future holds for you and your partner. What can you do when problems occur? It is simple. Praise God even when you do not know what will happen next. Praise Him for what He *will do.*

Such praise opens your life to some possibilities you may have never considered. By praising God, you not only become a risk taker, but you also become more aware of what He wants for you. This may be an uncomfortable idea for you. It may mean that you praise God in an unpleasant job situation or during a difficult financial position. It may mean praising God in spite of that taxing personal relationship you have in your family life. Perhaps you are troubled and perplexed about some situation. That is exactly when God wants you to praise Him.

When no answers or solutions seem to be available, and you face an immovable mountain, why not praise Him? What do you have to lose? You have already depleted your own answers. Why not admit it and look elsewhere for solutions and have an attitude of acceptance? Lloyd Ogilvie offers an informative thought along this line: "Consistent praise over a period of time conditions us to receive what the Lord has been waiting patiently to reveal to us or release for us."[1]

We readily thank people after the fact or if we are guaranteed they will help us out of the predicament according to our plan. To put our future in the hands of someone we cannot see or touch, however, and say, "Whatever You bring about in this matter, I praise You" is not typical. We resist, rebel and grate at the thought of praising God in every situation.

Think about it for a while before you discount the advice to give thanks "in all circumstances" (1 Thess. 5:18). You may have read and heard this passage presented dozens of times and perhaps ignored it. On occasion, we grasp at it during times of panic. What if this principle of praise became as regular as our daily eating routine? What might happen to us? It is worth a try.

First, consider who you are praising. Who is God to you? To some, God is a figment of a person's imagination. To others, a stone deity. A proper concept of God is basic to your existence and to practical daily Christian living. The best definition of God that has lasted through the years is found in the *Westminster Shorter Catechism*. In answer to the question, "What is God?" the reply is: "God is a Spirit, infinite, eternal, and unchangeable in his being, wisdom, power, holiness, justice, goodness and truth." Why were you created? To know God. What can bring you more contentment, joy, delight and peace than anything else? It is the knowledge of God, as the Scripture passage for today says.

When you and I rejoice in the Lord, we do not do it because we feel like it; it is an act of our wills, a commitment. When we rejoice in the Lord, we begin to see life from another viewpoint. Praise is our means of gaining a new perspective and new guidance for our bogged-down lives. You may be thinking you are too busy during the day to stop and praise God. That is just the time to do it, when you are too busy, fretful and overwhelmed. Stop, clear your mind and praise God. You will feel refreshed. Praising God in advance of a solution is an act of faith, a way of saying, "I don't know the outcome, but I am willing to trust." This will be a great boost for your marriage.[2]

Notes
1. Lloyd John Ogilvie, *God's Will in Your Life* (Eugene, Oreg: Harvest House Publishers, 1982), p. 136.
2. H. Norman Wright, *Making Peace with Your Past* (Grand Rapids: Fleming H. Revell, a Division of Baker Book House, 1985), p. 48, adapted.

The Path of Communication

A MAN OF KNOWLEDGE USES WORDS WITH RESTRAINT,

AND A MAN OF UNDERSTANDING IS EVEN-TEMPERED.

Proverbs 17:27

We had selected our destination—a lake miles away. It would take two hours of hiking to get there. As we left the parking area, we were suddenly faced with a choice of trails. Of the three leading into the mountain area, one seemed to be more traveled and better kept than the others. As we hiked along, we soon discovered that this was a well-traveled and central trail. From time to time a secondary trail branched out to a lake, mountain or high meadow area.

We passed more than 12 branching trails before we reached what we thought was our destination. Instead of finding the lake we were seeking, we had reached a rise overlooking three small but inviting lakes scattered about a basin. Our trail divided into three paths, each leading through the pines to one of these lakes. We now had a greater variety of available lakes for our fishing expedition.

Thinking back, we realized that our choice of the main path had given us a wide variety of options. No doubt we would have discovered one of the lakes we fished by taking one of the smaller-branching trails. But the well-worn trail gave access to many natural delights. Without it, our experiences would have been greatly limited.

One of the main paths that feeds the marital relationship is communication. Communication is the main artery that gives access to other avenues. "Without communication, the possibilities for a relationship become hopeless, the resources of the partners for the relationship are no longer available, the means for healing the hurts that previous communication may have caused are no longer present; and each, when he recovers from his need to justify himself and hurt the other, will find himself in a bottomless pit of loneliness from which he cannot be pulled except by the ropes of communication, which may or may not be capable of pulling him out again because of their weakened condition."[1]

Reuel Howe said: "If there is any one indispensable insight with which a young married couple should begin their life together, it is that they should try to keep open, at all cost, the lines of communication between them."[2]

Dr. David and Vera Mace painted the following picture of communication and marriage: "A marriage can be likened to a large house with many rooms to which a couple fall heir on their wedding day. Their hope is to use and enjoy these rooms, as we do the rooms in a comfortable home, so that they will serve the many activities that make up their shared life. But in many marriages, doors are found to be locked—they represent areas in the relationship which the couple are unable to explore together. Attempts to open these doors lead to failure and frustration. The right key cannot be found. So the couple resign themselves to living together in only a few rooms that can be opened easily, leaving the rest of the house, with all its promising possibilities, unexplored and unused.

"There is, however, a master key that will open every door. It is not easy to find. Or, more correctly, it has to be forged by the couple together, and this can be very difficult. It is the great art of effective marital communication."[3]

Is one pattern of communication better than others? Is one style more productive than others? Many helpful books have been written about this topic during the past few years. A much older book, however, provides the most comprehensive and helpful pattern of all. This book is called the Bible. You may want to read what is says. The following verses will help you as you begin your journey: James 3:2; 1 Peter 3:10; Proverbs 18:21; 21:23; 15:4; 25:15; Ephesians 4:15,25.

Notes
1. David and Vera Mace, *We Can Have Better Marriages If We Want Them* (Nashville: Abingdon Press, 1974), p. 99.
2. Reuel Howe, *Herein Is Love* (Valley Forge, Pa.: Judson Press, 1961), p. 100.
3. Mace, *We Can Have Better Marriages If We Want Them*, pp. 98-99.

You Can Have an Attitude

GIVE THANKS IN ALL CIRCUMSTANCES, FOR THIS IS
GOD'S WILL FOR YOU IN CHRIST JESUS.

1 Thessalonians 5:18

You have heard the expression, "That person has an attitude." It is usually said to denote a problem. But attitude can be a virtue!

Attitude. What is it? It is a choice we make to look at life a certain way. It determines the atmosphere of our homes and the way we interact with other people.

Some people claim they were born with gloomy dispositions. Perhaps some of your family members seem to have been born with an abundance of gratitude genes whereas others seem to be shortchanged. Some have a sore disposition whereas others can be ridiculously cheerful and grateful.

Yet we do not inherit gratitude genes from our parents. We *choose* to display gratitude. We can choose to be thankful and look for the best and the blessings rather than the defects. We can choose to search, discover and not take for granted what we have or experience. It will be especially important in your marriage.

Gratitude unexpressed is wasted. If kept private, its benefit is never fully experienced by you or others. A sense of gratitude can be infectious; it can affect the attitude of others.

We were probably taught to say, "Thank you." It is even more important to thank God for all we are, all we have and all in which we delight. Again and again the psalms say, "Oh, give thanks to the Lord" or "I will give thanks to the Lord."

Consider the following Scripture passages:

"Let the peace of Christ rule in your hearts, since as members of one body you were called to peace. And be thankful" (Col 3:15).

"Giving thanks to the Father, who has qualified you to share in the inheritance of the saints in the kingdom of light" (Col. 1:12).

"Do not be anxious about anything, but in everything, by prayer and petition, with thanksgiving, present your requests to God" (Phil. 4:6).

The apostle Paul told the church at Thessalonica: "Give thanks in all circumstances, for this is God's will for you in Christ Jesus" (1 Thess. 5:18).

Scripture tells us that thankfulness is a prerequisite for worship: "Enter his gates with thanksgiving and his courts with praise; give thanks" (Ps. 100:4).

For what are you thankful? Take a few moments and write your answer. Could it be that some gratitude needs expression in a phone call or a note? What about your parents, grandparents or other relatives? For what is your future partner thankful? I wonder what will happen when you look at your partner and say, "I'm so thankful for you"?

Perhaps you could ask your parents or partner today for what they are thankful. Never take one another for granted, but let everyone know your heartfelt thanks. If it is difficult to see for what you can be thankful, begin to look with new eyes—with God's perspective. Ask Him to illumine the eyes of your heart.

You Can Change

THE WORD OF GOD IS LIVING AND ACTIVE.
SHARPER THAN ANY DOUBLE-EDGED SWORD, IT
PENETRATES EVEN TO DIVIDING SOUL AND SPIRIT,
JOINTS AND MARROW; IT JUDGES THE THOUGHTS
AND ATTITUDES OF THE HEART.

Hebrews 4:12

"I can't change. I've tried and tried. Heaven only knows it's impossible. I'm stuck." Many people actually believe those words. They are frustrated with their efforts. They try not to get upset at others, or blow up, but they can't seem to change. They have   destructive habits. Yet God's Word emphatically says we *can* change.

One area in particular that is a source of turmoil for many of us is our thought lives. What goes on in our minds is often a battleground we would not want anyone to view if it were played on a video! We have negative thoughts about ourselves, friends, employers or employees and even our partners. We struggle with lust, envy, jealousy and pride. We know we want to change for the better, yet we do not seem to change much or as fast as we want.

You *will* change, however; you *can* change. You are in for a radical change. Scripture says that because the Holy Spirit dwells in your heart, you will be transformed: "We, who with unveiled faces all reflect the Lord's glory, are being transformed into his likeness with ever-increasing glory, which comes from the Lord, who is the Spirit" (2 Cor. 3:18).

Change *is* possible for those of us who are believers in Christ Jesus, because our faith is an inward transformation, not just an outward conformity. When Paul says, "My little children, of whom I travail in birth again until *Christ be formed in you*" (Gal. 4:19, *KJV*, emphasis added), he is telling us that we have to let Jesus Christ live *in* and *through* us.

In Ephesians 4:23,24, we are told to "be renewed in the spirit of your mind;...put on the new man, which after God is created in righteousness and true holiness" *(KJV)*. The new man has to be put on from the inside. We are able to put on the new man because God has placed Jesus Christ within us. We are to let Him work within us. That means we must give Him access to our memory banks and our past experiences that need to be relinquished.

Look again at Hebrews 4:12. The word "active" means "energize." God's Word energizes us for change. How? The apostle Paul says, "We demolish arguments and every pretension that sets itself up against the knowledge of God, and we take captive every thought to make it obedient to Christ" (2 Cor. 10:5).

Yet transformation takes time. It is slow. Sometimes you focus so much on what you want to become you fail to see the progress. If you have ever grown fruit trees or berries you know what I mean. At first some new growth appears on the plant, then a blossom turns into the fruit. Then the colors change. Although the fruit may have the right color, it is bitter if you pick it too soon. It has not become mature. You have to wait on it. Likewise, you have to wait on yourself.

As a child, perhaps you played a game called "Capture the Flag." As adults, we need to engage in capturing our thoughts. Why? Because that is usually where negative feelings begin and communication problems start.

How can we capture our thoughts? By memorizing Scripture. What change do you need to make that will make a difference in your upcoming marriage? What thoughts would you like to be rid of today? Write them down. Ask God to make you aware of when those thoughts pop into your mind. Write down the thoughts you would like to have in place of the old ones. Read them aloud several times a day. And watch out—it will put you on the road to change!

FIFTY-NINE

Don't Sweat the Small Stuff

A MAN'S WISDOM GIVES HIM PATIENCE; IT IS TO HIS
GLORY TO OVERLOOK AN OFFENSE.

Proverbs 19:11

How will you respond when your partner does any of the
following:

- Forgets to write down a phone message or forgets to
  phone about being 15 minutes late for dinner.
- Doesn't put down the garage door when leaving for
  work or doesn't note written checks in the register.
- Eats more ice cream than you would prefer or spends
  more time hammering away in the workshop than you
  would like.
- Talks on the telephone too much or thinks you need
  more exercise.
- Likes to go shopping, but never calls ahead to see if the
  store carries the product desired or hates to go shopping
  and never lends a hand in buying groceries or house-
  hold items.

This is small stuff that can become big stuff. In every marriage, each day produces many small offenses. You will need
to learn to ignore the little offenses to make your marriage
work. The more you attack every small infraction of your
self-styled rules and regulations, the less room you will find
for love and affection in your marriage. It helps to laugh
more and legislate less.

You need to be patient with one another. Humans are odd
creatures. Not only are our partners funny ducks at times,
but you, too, have many quirks that can grate on the nerves
of your partner. You have many weaknesses your spouse
will not see in the early days of your honeymoon. We have
many habits that can be taken as insensitivity. God's Word
offers some more advice, "So don't criticize each other any

more. Try instead to live in such a way that you will never make your brother stumble by letting him see you doing something he thinks is wrong" (Rom. 14:13, *TLB*).

Wisdom leads to patience—to letting the little offenses go. "A man's wisdom gives him patience; it is to his glory to overlook an offense" (Prov. 19:11). To grow in your marriage, you will need to grow in maturity and wisdom. Overlooking an offense is not the work of the spiritually immature. Each day couples have countless conflicts, most of which would never happen if people would let the little ones go. Pride, however, gets in the way.

Pride leads to impatience. Pride is the fruit of folly. Folly is the opposite of wisdom. Some people strut about, puffed up in their self-importance, pushing too hard and telling people off. It is better to be humble and let the little ones go. Don't sweat the small stuff. It is not worth it.

Notice the opening verse: "It is to his glory to overlook an offense"—the individual's glory, not God's glory. This is a rare occasion when glory is ascribed to people. The principle of overlooking offenses is so important to our Lord that He lets people receive glory when they do so. This is not the same kind of glory God receives; yet you or your partner can receive a kind of glory by letting the little ones go.

The secret to this principle is always to strive to raise the threshold of what you see as "little." *In other words, constantly try to let bigger and bigger offenses become smaller and smaller.*

If your partner's smallest offense that grates your nerves is not putting down the garage door, try putting it down yourself and letting it go. Is it really a major problem? If so, perhaps you could approach it differently.

SIXTY

A Marriage Benediction

TO HIM WHO IS ABLE TO KEEP YOU FROM FALLING
AND TO PRESENT YOU BEFORE HIS GLORIOUS PRES-
ENCE WITHOUT FAULT AND WITH GREAT JOY—TO THE
ONLY GOD OUR SAVIOR BE GLORY, MAJESTY, POWER
AND AUTHORITY, THROUGH JESUS CHRIST OUR LORD,
BEFORE ALL AGES, NOW AND FOREVERMORE! AMEN.

Jude 24,25

A benediction is usually prayed at the conclusion of the wedding service. You may want to use the following benediction, compiled from various sources:

May your marriage bring you all the fulfillment a marriage should bring and may the Lord give you patience, tolerance and understanding. May it be full of joy and laughter, as well as comfort and support. May you discover the true depth of love through loving one another.

Remember that every burden is easier to carry when you have the shoulders of two instead of one. When you are weary and discouraged, look to Jesus to refresh and strengthen you.

May you always need one another—not so much to fill your emptiness, as to help you to know your fullness. May you always need one another, but not out of weakness. Rejoice in and praise one another's uniqueness, for God is the creator of both male and female and differences in personality.

Be faithful to one another in your thoughts and deeds and above all, be faithful to Jesus. May you see the marriage bed as an altar of grace and pleasure. May you remember that each time you speak to one another you are talking to someone that God has claimed and told, "You are very special." View and treat your partner as one who was created in the image of God. Remember that you are not to hold your partner captive, but to give freedom to become all that God wants the person to be. May you then embrace and hold one another, but not encircle one another.

May God renew your minds so you look to draw out the best and the potential in one another. Look for things to praise, never take one another for granted, often say, "I love you" and take no notice of little faults. Affirm one another, defer to one another and believe in your partner. If you have differences that push you apart, may both of you have good sense enough to take the first step back. May the words "You're right," "Forgive me" and "I forgive you" be close at hand.

Thank You, heavenly Father, for Your presence here with us and for Your blessing upon this marriage.

In Jesus' name,

Amen.